SELFLESS LOVE

SELFLESS LOVE

Beyond the Boundaries
of Self and Other

Ellen Birx

WISDOM PUBLICATIONS • BOSTON

Wisdom Publications
199 Elm Street
Somerville, MA 02144 USA
www.wisdompubs.org

Library of Congress
Cataloging-in-Publication Data
Birx, Ellen.
  Selfless love : beyond the boundaries of self and other / Ellen Birx.
    pages cm
  Includes bibliographical references
and index.
  ISBN 1-61429-075-X (pbk. : alk.
paper)—ISBN 978-1-61429-094-0
(eBook)
  1. Meditation. 2. Love—Religious
aspects. I. Title.
  BL627.B54 2014
  205'.677—dc23

ISBN 978-1-61429-075-9

18 17 16 15 14
5 4 3 2 1

Cover design by Phil Pascuzzo.
Interior design by Gopa&Ted2.
Set in 11.25/14.94.
Author photo courtesy of
Livingston-Smith Photography Inc.

Wisdom Publications' books are
printed on acid-free paper and meet
the guidelines for permanence
and durability of the Production
Guidelines for Book Longevity of the
Council on Library Resources.

Printed in the United States
of America.

This book was produced with
environmental mindfulness. We
have elected to print this title on 30%
PCW recycled paper. As a result, we
have saved the following resources: 9
trees, 4 million BTUs of energy, 802
lbs. of greenhouse gases, 4,352 gallons
of water, and 291 lbs. of solid waste.
For more information, please visit
our website, www.wisdompubs.org.
This paper is also FSC certified. For
more information, please visit www.
fscus.org.

To my teacher
Roshi Robert Jinsen Kennedy

Table of Contents

Introduction: You Are Love

THE WORD *love*, like the word *god*, is dangerous—yet I hold on to it. Love is not something you have or don't have; it's what you are. You are love. You are God's love. Nothing can separate you from this love because it is what you are.

There is no separate self that is apart from love, apart from the world, apart from the absolute, but we have grown up with the worldview that we are independent, individual selves. Along with the illusion of a separate self come fear, anxiety, defensiveness, and the loneliness of a self-centered life. We find ourselves longing for love to quench the deprivation caused by the sense of a separate self. The longing for love will only be satisfied when we see through the construct of self and experience selfless love, the only true love there is. My hope is that as you read this book, you will fall deeply in love. This of course takes trust—in love, in God—and self-surrender.

Throughout this book the word *god* is used in addition to alternatives such as *being, presence, ultimate reality, great mystery, godhead, absolute,* or *infinite,* in order to renew and reclaim the word. Often *god* is avoided because it has been so widely used in concrete and overly anthropomorphic ways. However, the Pew U.S. Religious Landscape Survey tells us that 92 percent of the people in the United States believe in God or a universal spirit. This same poll reveals that 75 percent of Buddhists, frequently thought not to believe in God, replied "Yes" to the question "Do you believe in God or a universal spirit?"

Shodo Harada Roshi, a well-respected Zen Master, is an example of a Buddhist who uses the word *god* and says that people who are able to believe in God, and not just science and technology, are blessed. In the documentary *The Man on Cloud Mountain* he discusses care for the dying at Enso House, the hospice he founded in Washington State, and suggests that caregivers have an attitude of prayer, saying, "Without prayer, life is little more than eating, sleeping, and making a living; with prayer, life is illuminated by the light of God. At Enso House we are trying to provide a place where hospice workers and residents alike can face death with a sense of the sacred." With a sense of the sacred, compassionate action is illuminated by God's love and by your loving actions, which are one reality.

In this book the word *god* is being used in a nondualistic way. It connotes that our discussion is not limited to the material or secular world but rather includes the spiritual or sacred. It acknowledges God's presence in marvelous, ordinary, everyday life. I chose to use the word *god*, risking that some will be turned away by it. However, when I considered other words, I found that God remained the elephant in the room. At the same time, it is important to emphasize that the God we are talking about here is not a person or thing. God is ineffable, unknowable, and way beyond words, concepts, and images. Indeed, this *not knowing* is essential for the intimate experience of God's functioning in the world. Words cannot explain God, but they can be helpful to evoke and expand our human capacity to be more sensitive to God's presence in our lives.

The word *love* is equally elusive. Volumes have been written by philosophers, theologians, and psychologists about different kinds of love, how to find it, and how to sustain it. Rather than categorizing types of love, the focus of this book is on seeing through the separate self and thereby opening to unbounded love. But insight into selflessness is not enough; it is just a beginning. Ongoing moment-by-moment practice is needed to remain attentive to the habitual patterns and conditioning that continuously arise and block selfless love.

This is why, at the outset, instructions for wordless meditation are provided, and the daily practice of meditation is encouraged, so you can see beyond words (even wonderful words like *god* and *love*), beyond thoughts, and beyond self, to directly experience the life and love that you are. Meditation helps you be alert and aware of conditioned patterns, and allows those patterns to dissipate, opening the way to selfless love. Wordless meditation helps you see through your self-image and through images of God that you have inherited or created. In the light of awareness, images dissolve, and the direct perception of *what is* becomes unobstructed and clear. New possibilities for living and loving arise.

God's love
Selfless compassionate action
Not separate realities
One sacred act
Healing yourself and others
In wholeness
Now and forever
Love prevails

The Basics of Meditation

Why Meditate?

FROM TIME TO TIME my grandchildren ask me, "Grandma, why do you meditate?" Often this question comes when I ask my husband to watch them for twenty-five minutes while I do my evening meditation. They want to know why it's so important that I take time to do it every day, especially when there are other fun things to be doing with them. I try to explain in a way a child can understand. Usually I say, "Meditation is a kind of prayer." They are satisfied with this answer and seem to appreciate the sacred nature of this time set aside.

This answer works for them, and for me it is the most honest answer. Ever since I first started meditating about forty years ago, I have viewed meditation as a way to be more present and open to God. My reason for meditating has always been spiritual, and meditation has been a labor of love.

These days many people begin meditation for other reasons, such as improving their physical or mental health and well-being. In many medical centers around the world meditation is being used for stress management, and there is a large body of research supporting its effectiveness. We now have a greater understanding of the integral relationship between body and mind. The power of the mind to affect the body is being applied to treat conditions like high blood pressure and chronic pain.

As neuroscientists study the effects of meditation on brain structure and function they are expanding our scientific knowledge regarding neuroplasticity. In a recent article in the AARP magazine, older adults are encouraged to include meditation, along with healthy eating and exercise, in their daily routines to prevent dementia.

Many people are learning to meditate in their psychotherapist's office. Meditation is being incorporated into new models of psychotherapy such as Acceptance and Commitment Therapy (ACT), Dialectical Behavioral Therapy (DBT), and Mindfulness-Based Cognitive Therapy (MBCT). DBT integrates cognitive-behavioral strategies with mindfulness skills, derived from Zen meditation, to help clients participate in life with awareness and behave more effectively. Mindfulness is a way for clients to be more present in the moment, rather than overburdened by the past or consumed by worries about the future. MBCT was developed to prevent relapses of depression; it combines cognitive therapy and mindfulness meditation to help clients gain a wider perspective on their thoughts, feelings, and physical sensations, thereby improving their mood. In the ACT model, the therapist facilitates the client's movement toward a more flexible view of the self as ongoing awareness and as context. In this model, "self" is not a thing; it is immaterial, spiritual, interconnected, and compassionate toward self and others. Research supports the effectiveness of these new models of psychotherapy in treating depression and anxiety.

Therapists also benefit from meditation. Like patients, they too can learn the art of being fully present; "presence" is the healing power of what they do and is a great asset for all caregivers. Meditation is also a way for therapists and caregivers to care for themselves as a foundation for caring for others. As a nurse, meditation helps me connect with patients on a deep human level and stay fully present, calm, and sensitive while accompanying patients through birth, life-threatening illness, recovery, and death.

When I began Zen meditation, I was attracted by the natural beauty, simplicity, and peacefulness of Zen gardens and meditation halls. The exquisite, uncluttered environments called me into a place of calm and serenity. The calm of meditation is a welcome antidote to the hectic pace of modern life. It is a chance to take a break from multitasking and pay attention to one thing at a time—sitting, breathing, walking, eating, or sleeping. It is a time just to be a human being alive on this earth. Meditation is like a pressure valve that releases the tension of driving in heavy traffic and constantly learning new computer programs. In the alert, balanced posture of meditation, muscles soften and new life is breathed into you. Powerful reasons for me to meditate are to decompress, simplify, unclutter, and experience again that I am not a machine; I am a human being. Meditation is an expression of my humanity and my unity with the earth and all its creatures.

On a mental level, meditation is a time to clean house. There is a reality television show called *Hoarding: Buried Alive* that depicts the lives of people who are on the brink of eviction or health crisis because they have filled their homes with things, sometimes up to the ceiling, with only a small path to get through each room. It shows the hoarders experiencing extreme anxiety and panic attacks when asked to part with any of their things. They resist letting go of anything, even at the risk of losing home, health, and family. Watching the show you think to yourself, "How could anyone live like that? I could never live like that." However, in meditation sometimes you find that you have filled your mind with so many thoughts, opinions, plans, stories, and images that there is no space left. You may have a hard time letting go of all this mental clutter. You may even notice feelings of anxiety as you try to let go of some of your cherished ideas about yourself, others, and life itself. Meditation is a way to stop the habit of mental hoarding and regain some spaciousness and mental clarity. It is like cleaning house and letting in a breath of fresh air.

Meditation is enlivening. It is like hitting the refresh button on the computer. You get up from meditation feeling new, vital, fresh, and sensitive. In meditation you open to a natural sense of peace, love, and joy. You are filled with gratitude and glad to be alive. This is important in a world where depression is all too prevalent and suicide all too common. When you take a break from incessant doing, and make time just to be, there is time and space for innocence, wonder, and awe.

We find this in the Christian tradition in the story of Martha and Mary. Mary sits fully present near Jesus—full of wonder and awe. Martha complains that Mary is just sitting there and not helping her as she works to prepare the meal and take care of the guests. Jesus responds that Mary has made the better choice. He is not saying that Mary is right and Martha is wrong; it is really not a matter of right and wrong. We are all both Martha and Mary. Too often our tendency is to be busy doing all that needs to be done in life. As a result of all this busyness, we, like Martha, may find ourselves tired, complaining, and distancing ourselves from others. We need to take time to sit down, be fully present, and experience the wonder, joy, and love that is offered.

In Eastern traditions the highest intention for meditating is to gain insight, wisdom, or enlightenment. However, this is often accompanied by a warning that wisdom alone is not enough; it must be embodied in compassionate action. Meditation is for liberation of the human spirit, your own and others'. In the final picture of the famous Zen oxherding pictures, which depict ten stages of spiritual development, we see the spiritual person returning to the marketplace, in ragged clothes, to mingle among the people and lend a helping hand.

Grandma, why do you meditate?
Meditation is a kind of prayer.
It helps me experience that God is near,
that God is right here.
God's breath is my breath.

When I am very silent and still
I hear every little sound—
a cricket, a birdsong,
the refrigerator turning on and off,
rain on the roof and running down the gutter pipes
into the earth,
a car swishing by on the wet road.

I see clearly too—
light growing brighter as night turns to day,
patterns in the grain of the hardwood floor,
the color of dawn.

During meditation I see
how often my mind is full of thoughts,
my body full of feelings,
rushing through life on a giant roller coaster

up and down, up and down,
holding on for dear life.

Meditation is a chance to get off the roller coaster,
slow down for a while,
feel calm and peaceful—
as my breath glides
in and out, in and out—
just breathing,
paying attention to life here and now.

I feel my heartbeat,
the heartbeat of the whole world,
not separate from grass, trees,
mountains, and sky.

I hear the laughing and crying of the whole world
like one body
with all people who breath and eat and grow.
I know I am not alone.

How to Meditate

WORDLESS MEDITATION is simple and easy to learn. There are three essentials: posture, breathing, and paying attention.

When you meditate, you get out of your head and into your whole body—so the posture of your body is important. Buddha statues have become very popular lately in interior design, and I think it is not just because of the peace and serenity that they convey. The straight, alert posture is a direct demonstration of human dignity. When sitting in meditation the back is straight and the ears are in line with the shoulders. You don't slouch or lean against the wall, sofa, or chair. Although this posture may be challenging at first, very quickly most people find their balance in this, and correct posture begins to feel better than slouching. When the back is straight, the mind is more likely to be calm and alert. This erect posture carries over into the rest of the day in the way you sit, stand, and walk. It is healthful, graceful, and elegant.

This straight-backed posture can be accomplished on a chair, on a meditation cushion, or on a meditation bench. On a meditation cushion, the legs can be arranged in a full lotus, a half lotus, or in the Burmese position: one foot pulled in against the cushion and the other foot on the floor close in front of the first foot. In all three of these positions, the knees are in contact with the floor. Whichever position you prefer, you place your "sit bones" on the front of the cushion and your two knees on the floor, forming a stable tripod base. If you use a bench, the sit bones on the bench and the two knees on the floor form the tripod. In a chair, you sit forward on the chair, not leaning against the back of the chair, with your sit bones on the front of the chair and your two feet planted firmly on the floor to form the tripod base. Some people are more flexible than others, so select the position that is best for you, remembering that you can be just as alert and awake on a chair as on a bench or cushion. I encourage you to experiment with various positions and different size cushions, chairs, and benches.

While sitting on the front of the meditation cushion, bench, or chair, it helps to tilt the pelvis forward a bit, which results in slightly increasing the natural curve of the lower back. This allows for the back to straighten up taller and the belly to come forward, soft and open. The shoulders are back and dropped down. The head is directly over the shoulders as if looking straight ahead. The eyes are open but cast down at the floor two to three feet in front of you. The eyes look down, but the head is not tilted downward. Keeping your eyes open during meditation helps you remain awake and present, right here and now. If your eyes are closed, you are more likely to become drowsy or drift off into daydreaming.

The posture described above sets you up for relaxed, natural abdominal breathing. The belly is unconstricted so it can expand and diminish freely with each inhalation and exhalation. When a baby lies sleeping you can watch his or her little belly rise with inhalation and sink with exhalation. That is how you naturally breathe. In meditation you don't try to breathe in any particular way. You just let your attention be on your belly rising and falling as you naturally breathe.

Most of us have spent time standing by the ocean watching the waves roll in one after the other. Are all of the waves the same size? No; some are larger and some are smaller. Some roll in around your ankles and some get you wet up to your knees. It's the same with natural breathing. One breath after another rhythmically rolls in, but some breaths are a little bigger or smaller than others. This is fine. Don't try to regulate the breath—making the breaths all the same size, or making the breath rate faster or slower. Just let your awareness rest on the belly rising and falling as you breathe naturally.

Breath is life itself, and you live life breath by breath in the present moment. Just this breath, just this moment! When you begin thinking, thought carries you off into the past or into the future and you are no longer present right here and now. Sitting in meditation, a thought may come up, such as, "What will I have for a snack this evening?"

As soon as you become aware that you are thinking, just let go of the thought and bring your attention back to your breathing—to your awareness of the belly rising and falling. You don't need to try to push thoughts out of your head; just don't add to them. When you find yourself thinking about an evening snack, let go of the thought and come back to your breathing, rather than mentally scanning your refrigerator and constructing a sandwich in your mind.

Thoughts may enter your mind a hundred times during a session of meditation. You simply let go of the thought and return your attention to your breathing. At times you may become lost in thought and several minutes may go by before you even realize you are thinking. This is not a problem. When you realize you are thinking, just let go of the stream of thoughts, and bring your attention back to the breathing. What you don't do in meditation is decide to use the time for problem-solving, storytelling, or your usual mental dialogue. What you don't do in meditation is intentionally think or daydream. The point of meditation is to take a break from your usual ways of thinking that tend to dominate your life and block other ways of being alive.

Outside of meditation there is nothing wrong with thinking. It serves a purpose—it allows you to function in the world. The problem is that thinking takes over. Meditation is a way to expand your repertoire and increase your flexibility in living. Meditation is not limited to thinking about anything. It is not about figuring anything out or fixing anything. It is about seeing life just as it is and being who you really are. It is about uncovering and seeing clearly. Meditation is an intuitive opening.

Recent neuroscience research has identified different areas of the brain that are activated during different types of meditation. James Austin, who is a medical doctor and neurophysiologist, has researched and practiced Zen meditation for many years. In his book *Meditating Selflessly* he points out that focused-attention meditation is a voluntary process that activates the upper regions of the parietal and frontal lobes on both sides of the brain. Whereas in open-awareness meditation, which is a more receptive and involuntary process, areas lower down in the right temporoparietal junction and the right inferior frontal cortex are activated. He emphasizes that these two different meditation processes are complementary and that the meditator typically starts out with focused attention and then cycles back and forth between focused attention and open awareness during a session of meditation.

I began my discussion of "How to Meditate" with directions for focused attention on the breath. This is what you *do* during meditation. You pay attention to your breathing, to your abdomen rising and falling, and if your mind wanders off in thought, you let go of the thought and gently bring your attention back to your breathing. As you become more experienced in meditation, you don't always need to come specifically back to the breath but can just let go of the thoughts and come back to your posture or to your whole body sitting straight and tall. Sometimes your awareness becomes clear without thought. The senses are open to sounds and sensations—the sound of rain or cars swishing by out in the street, the feeling of a cool breeze on your skin, the patterns of light and dark shadows on the floor or wall. As long as you are not thinking, sit in this open awareness. When thoughts begin to come back into your mind, don't join them, just bring your attention back to your breath. In this way you move back and forth between what you *do* in meditation (let go of thought and pay attention to your breathing or posture) and what *happens* (your awareness becomes clear and open). Remember, open awareness is not something you do; it is involuntary and happens all on its own.

Meditating like this cultivates insight into selflessness. The dissolution of the sense of a separate self is not something you can make happen. With patience, selflessness will be revealed.

Meditation can be viewed as a type of prayer, as silent, wordless prayer. In meditation as prayer, we don't think about God, or spiritual ideas. These are thoughts. God is beyond all thoughts, words, concepts, and images. We simply sit, present, open, listening, alert, and awake. This is the prayer sung in Psalm 46:10: "Be still, and know that I am God."

It's good to start out with ten or fifteen minutes each day until you establish a regular daily practice. Then gradually increase up to twenty-five minutes each morning or evening, or both. A pattern of daily practice is more beneficial than meditating for a long time one day and not at all other days. Creating a meditation space that is free of clutter, with your cushion, bench, or chair set up waiting for you, is a good reminder. This may be a spare room or a corner of your bedroom or living room. Sitting with a group once a week and attending periodic retreats are also helpful to energize and deepen your meditation practice.

Several times a year our Zen group, New River Zen Community, gets together for a day of silence and meditation. We do periods of sitting meditation alternating with walking meditation and take breaks for tea and lunch. One beautiful spring day, as we sat together in round after round of meditation, I was thrilled by a magnificent orchestra of birdsong. The birdsong was not just out in the trees outside the windows; it rippled through my body as I sat alert and open. It became crystal clear to me that becoming lost in thought was just like a switch turning off the birdsong. I didn't hear it at all until I realized I was thinking and let go of the thought, becoming alert and present again, just breathing. This turned on the switch and the beautiful birdsong was heard again. The awareness and presence we practice during meditation can be practiced outside of meditation as well so we are not lost in thought and daydreaming, missing the birdsong and life itself.

Now I'll be silent
Not let my thoughts drown out the singing bird
And hear Your voice beyond all words
With every cell
Awake
To hear You sing
And be Your singing

Experiencing Selflessness

No Self, No Center

IN THE UNITED STATES, we have grown up in a culture that places great value on positive self-esteem and a strong sense of individual identity. We in turn have cultivated this in our children with frequent praise and positive reinforcement of their strengths and accomplishments. We rejoice over each developmental milestone they reach on the road to greater independence. In some cultures this is not the case. In many Asian cultures self-esteem and autonomy are not emphasized, but rather living in harmonious relationships with others and bringing honor to the family through hard work and academic excellence are valued. Alternative perceptions of self have the potential to enhance our understanding of this important aspect of human development.

A clear sense of self—of your needs, likes, wants, and values—is essential for functioning well in the world. However, this sense of self can get out of balance and lead some people to develop an inflated ego and sense of entitlement. Whereas others end up with low self-esteem, out of touch with their strengths, ambivalent about their identity, floundering, and depressed by unmet expectations.

What exactly is this self in need of balance? Is it your body? Body image plays a major role in how a person feels about him- or herself. Being slim, strong, and beautiful is greatly valued in our culture and is an asset in many of life's circumstances. Often physical appearance can have an undue influence on self-esteem. I notice this each time I step on the scale. If I've lost a pound or two, I feel happy and successful. It's an instant mood booster. On the other hand, if I've gained weight, I feel discouraged. My efforts to eat healthfully and exercise regularly have not paid off, or I've indulged a few too many times, and I'm not happy about it. It's sad that the numbers that pop up on my digital scale exert such an immediate effect on my mood. Even though I am able to view my weight in the larger scheme of things, and not dwell on it, at the same time the disappointment and its effect on how I feel about myself are there, and I acknowledge these thoughts and feelings. Luckily, despite the undue emphasis placed on weight and physical appearance in our culture, most people recognize that they are more than the body.

For many people self-esteem extends beyond their physical form to include the things they own. They feel better about themselves if they have attractive clothing, a nice home, and a fancy car. Some people are collectors and get satisfaction, at least temporarily, each time they acquire a new addition to their collections. Some collect less tangible things such as degrees, awards, or achievements. The growing collection shores up and expands their sense of self. However, on some level, most people recognize that they are more than their possessions, tangible or intangible.

So what is the self if it is not just the body or what you own or accomplish? And where is the self? Is it inside of you somewhere? Is the self in the head where an ongoing commentary about life is going on? Or perhaps the self is the commentary itself, the story of you that you are telling. Is the self in the heart, since that is where your deepest emotions reside? Perhaps the self is your kindness or the good that you do. Is the self your awareness or self-awareness? If so where is the self when you are in deep sleep? Is the self in your genes, since they contain the information about many of your unique characteristics such as your fingerprints, temperament, and predispositions? Or are you both nature and nurture, inseparable from the context in which you live, which includes your family, your friends, your job, your culture, your circumstances, and your world?

It's impossible to locate the self and point to it directly. Whatever you point to, there is always the sense that there is more to it than that. This is because the self does not exist as a thing but rather a coming together of many aspects, internal and external, and it is constantly changing moment by moment.

Some say you must go deep within to find your true self at your center or core. Where is your center? Is it inside your body? Is it your center of gravity, deep down in your lower abdomen? Is it your solar plexus? Is it in your heart region? Is it in your head, deep down in your brain? Or is it deep within the shifting sands of your interior world of thoughts, emotions, and sensations? You can't find it because there is no center of the self, since there is no self that exists as a separate entity.

You may say, "But what about my core values and spiritual beliefs?" Are your most deeply held values and spiritual beliefs the self, the true self, the center, or the core? Or are they thoughts and feelings you hold dearly about what is most important in life? There is no center of yourself, and you are not the center of the universe. Not being self-centered is a value shared by many religious traditions. This is not a new idea, but I am encouraging you to experience it directly as a reality rather than just a thought or ideal.

Though you search and search, you cannot come up with something that is the self, or the center of the self, because there is no separate thing called a self and therefore there is no center of it. If you take the self apart, you see that the self is not limited to any of the pieces. Although some types of meditation are called "centering," the type of meditation described in this book is more of a *decentering*. Ideas such as self versus other, center versus periphery, and inside versus outside are not reinforced. We see through the limitations of these dichotomies. This is not just an intellectual exercise; you can't just read about it in a book and say, "Oh, that makes sense. I get it." In the stillness and quiet of meditation you inquire deeply and experience directly for yourself what remains when all parts of the self are let go. What remains when everything that is not you falls away? You will come face-to-face with your original self, without beginning and without end, without center and without periphery. Deconstructing the self is not the point; the point is what is revealed when the sense of a separate self is allowed to dissolve completely.

When you see that self is not a thing and that there is no center to it or to you, you move beyond being self-centered and are liberated to live selflessly. Living selflessly does not mean that you don't have a healthy sense of your unique qualities as a human being, or that you don't have the ego needed to function in the world. It means that you are not limited by a narrow or rigid view of self. You are no longer dominated by the ego. The ego is like the wizard in *The Wizard of Oz*. Once the curtain is pulled back, you see that the one who has been pulling the strings all along is not as powerful and mysterious as you thought. You see right through your limited ego-self. You experience its dynamic, fluid nature. Seeing that the self is not a fixed entity opens new ways of being in the world. Without a fixed sense of self, you move through life with the fluidity of water and the freedom of wind.

Who is not a thing?
You are who is not a thing.

Who is the one and who are the many?
You are who and who is all you see.

Who sees?
Who sees who.
Who breathes?
Who breathes who.

Who makes the thunder in the sky?
Who rumbles.

Who am I when I'm sound asleep?
Who sleeps.

Who was I before I was born?
Who is the unborn.

When the body is gone who remains?
Right now who remains?
Who remains.
You are who.

You Are Not Your Thoughts or Feelings

M EDITATION IS a time to take a break from thinking. It's not that you don't have any thoughts
during meditation but rather that you don't intentionally
engage in thinking. As you sit in silence, you notice your
usual patterns of thoughts arising in the form of internal
commentary on what is happening: "Gee, it's noisy. Who's
mowing their lawn just as I sit down to meditate?" You
find yourself judging your meditation: "I'm really rest-
less today. I should be more peaceful than this. I must be
doing something wrong." You find yourself judging your
behavior outside of meditation: "I don't know why I got
so upset with her. I wish I'd kept my cool and not let her
know how much she was irritating me." Sometimes you
become lost in memories or start planning for the future.
Sometimes creative thoughts arise and you are tempted to
write a poem or a whole novel. The fact that so many different types of thoughts enter your mind while meditating
is not a problem as long as you make the choice to let them
go and gently bring your attention back to your breathing.
You cannot control the thoughts that enter your mind,

but you can choose whether or not to entertain them and invite them to stay.

The presence of thoughts in the mind is not the problem; the problem is the tendency to identify with your thoughts or view them as reality. When you think to yourself, "I'm overwhelmed" or "I'm bored," or "I'm depressed," you are making the feeling into a thing that is real and you are identifying with the thought and feeling. The practice of meditation is to see the changing nature of thoughts and feelings and not hold on to them or identify with them.

During meditation you are alert and awake yet not absorbed in thinking. Continually letting go of thoughts opens up the space and clarity to experience who it is that you are beyond thought. You see that you are more than the sum of your thoughts.

There is a great liberation that comes with this realization. If you identify with your thoughts, you are bound by them. When you see through and beyond your thoughts, and experience the full reality of who you are, the small, constricted self that you have created with your thoughts is seen through and this transparency sets you free.

Cognitive therapy has helped many people take a step in the direction of seeing that they are not their thoughts but rather the author of their thoughts. In cognitive therapy you learn how your thoughts affect the way you feel and how your feelings affect your behaviors. By identifying negative, distorted thoughts that enter your mind when you encounter difficult situations, and by examining the accuracy and usefulness of these thoughts, you are able to move on to construct more balanced and helpful thoughts. Balanced thoughts lead to a decrease in negative feelings and an increase in effective behaviors. One day in the class I teach on mental health nursing, we were practicing cognitive therapy techniques. At the end of the session the students, who were juniors in college, found the approach so useful for themselves they said, "Why couldn't we learn this sooner? We could have really used this in high school!" They thought it would have helped them cope with how upset they felt when peers said things that were hurtful, left them out, let them down, or gossiped about them.

Newer psychotherapy approaches that incorporate insights from meditation practice, such as Mindfulness-Based Cognitive Therapy (MBCT), don't focus on changing the content of negative, distorted thoughts. Instead the emphasis is on changing your *relationship* to your thoughts, feelings, and physical sensations, by nonjudgmentally paying attention to them during meditation as they arise in the present moment. Through awareness of thoughts, feelings, and sensations arising moment by moment, you see that thoughts, feelings, and sensations are not facts. They are events emerging within your broader field of awareness. They are not who you are.

In MBCT, you learn to decenter from negative thoughts, feelings, and sensations by viewing them within a broader perspective. Decentering is not detachment, dissociation, or repression, which distance you from life. Awareness, during meditation, and during daily life, creates the space to allow these thoughts and feelings to be befriended rather than pushed away. Difficult thoughts, feelings, and sensations are acknowledged and allowed to be present; yet with expanded awareness, they no longer dominate. Rather than trying to fix them, you allow them to be present as part of a larger reality. You see their changing nature and are able to move with them as they arise and subside.

Acceptance and Commitment Therapy (ACT) is another mindfulness-based psychotherapy model that uses different terms for similar processes. In ACT the term *defusion* is used instead of the term *decentering* to refer to becoming aware that your thoughts are just thoughts and not reality itself. Rather than focusing on changing the content of distorted thoughts, as is the emphasis in cognitive therapy, you step back from those thoughts; you become aware of your experience in the present moment and how the experience is expressed in words and thoughts. The goal is to free you from the domination of thinking, of living only in your head, stuck in problem-solving mode. Openness and cognitive flexibility are fostered to help you break through the illusion that words and thoughts are reality itself—to help you stop mistaking them for the richness of life.

The goal of mindfulness-based therapies is not to do away with thinking. The ability to think logically and critically is a great asset for functioning in the world and for creating a more humane life for yourself and others.

Creative thinking allows you to envision better alternatives and work toward them. Yet thinking, planning, and problem-solving are not the only way to exist; your life can be balanced and enriched by learning how to let go of thinking and get in touch with just being.

Meditation is a way to experience being. Meditation puts thinking into perspective and introduces you to another way of being present and aware in the midst of your life.

Sitting in meditation, you are open not only to thoughts but also to feelings and physical sensations. Waves of happiness, sadness, anger, affection, or hurt wax and wane. You develop sensitivity to feelings as they first arise. You come to know them in their subtlety and in their intensity. You directly experience their changing nature; what comes up also goes back down again. When you just feel the feeling, without fueling the story line that keeps it going, it more quickly subsides. You experience directly that you are not the ever-changing landscape of your feelings.

This enhanced awareness of your feelings carries over into daily life. You more quickly notice when a coworker's comment elicits a feeling of irritation within you. You develop the sensitivity to recognize the feeling more quickly, before reacting inappropriately. The early recognition of the feeling arising within you buys you the time to choose how you want to respond, rather that reacting off the cuff, and escalating the situation.

Sometimes, sitting in the stillness of meditation, feelings take form in your body as a pain or an itch. Like emotions, physical sensations also tend to wax and wane, building to an almost unbearable intensity at times, and then changing or shifting to a different sensation, or going away completely. If you resist the urge to move or scratch, and enter into the sensation with interest and curiosity, you notice its qualities changing moment by moment. Meditation is not just a way to get to know how your mind works, with its intellect and emotions; you become intimate with your whole body.

Meditation is an intuitive process. When you are not absorbed in your same old thoughts, ruminating about your feelings, or avoiding physical sensations, there is space for something new to emerge. In *The Record of Transmitting the Light*, Zen Master Keizan describes what emerges as "alert, clear, and originally bright." You see that your thoughts are not fixed entities that can be fixed. You are not a fixed entity that can be fixed. You are not limited to, or by, your thoughts, feelings, and sensations. You are alert, clear, and bright. You are an inseparable manifestation of the whole, changing moment by moment.

Subtle
Refined
Clear
I too am insubstantial

Before words
Beyond thoughts
Already gone
Yet still here
I am

There Is No Witness or Observer

WHEN YOU SIT down in meditation, paying attention to your breathing, you quickly become aware of how many thoughts come into your mind. With these thoughts come emotions, sometimes felt mildly in the background and sometimes more intensely, perhaps accompanied by tears or the urge to laugh right out loud. You also notice bodily sensations such as aching in your shoulder or itching as a stray hair tickles the side of your face. You notice all of this naturally, without the need to intentionally observe thoughts, feelings, or physical sensations.

Although you start out intending to pay attention to your breathing, you do not *observe* your breathing. You simply let your attention rest on it and gently return your attention when it wanders off in thought. You are aware and alert, just breathing naturally. You are already breathing and have been breathing since the day you were born. Don't separate from the act of breathing itself by creating an observer.

The same is true for thinking. There is no need to observe your thoughts, thereby reinforcing the sense of yourself as an observer. Although in some types of meditation there is an emphasis on observing or monitoring your thoughts, it can be divisive and block the experience of the undivided wholeness of life. Zen Master Josho Pat Phelan suggests just dropping thoughts during meditation and returning to the direct experience of the present moment, such as the breath in the lower abdomen. She warns against using one part of your mind to police or monitor another part of your mind. Monitoring narrows and constricts awareness and openness of mind.

In the book *Thoughts without a Thinker*, Mark Epstein integrates Buddhist psychology and meditation with psychoanalytic theory and therapy. From a Buddhist perspective, there is no separate self and thus no separate "you" who is the thinker. The fact that thoughts arise does not mean that something called a thinker exists as a separate entity. Thoughts occur in the context of all the factors that come together in the present moment to comprise the particular manifestation of the whole that is your own unique reality, but the sense of yourself as a separate thing that exists across time, as a thinker, is an illusion.

In the English language we use the words *observing* and *observer*, *monitoring* and *monitor*, *thinking* and *thinker*; however, we speak of *awareness* and *being aware*. There is no activity called "awaring" and no word "awarer." As the phrase "being aware" implies, we don't do awareness, we are aware. Awareness is not something we do, it is what we are. When we drop all the thoughts, concept, words, judgments, and opinions that divide all that is into categories, we experience undivided awareness.

However, observing can be a helpful step toward awareness in the context of psychotherapy. Dialectical Behavioral Therapy (DBT) teaches core mindfulness skills that include observing, describing, and participating. In this system, *observing* and *describing* are skills learned to reach the goal of participating with awareness. Marsha Linehan, the developer of DBT, says they are steps useful when learning a new behavior, such as playing a musical instrument or driving a car, or when a problem is encountered that requires change. Observing, for instance, involves paying attention to the details of the experience. In the case of learning to play guitar, you need to become aware of the angle and pressure of your fingertips on the strings, and the quality of sound that results from each position of the fingers. Observing requires you to step back from the activity itself to notice the various aspects of the activity. When we become experienced at playing the guitar we drop the observing and play fluidly. Describing, then, is a core mindfulness skill that involves using words to express your experiences. Words are labels that allow you to communicate and give you a sense of being more in control of your emotions and sensations. An aspect of the mindfulness skill of describing is learning that thoughts and words are not reality itself. This releases you from being unduly influenced or burdened by negative or distorted thoughts.

For Linehan, participating is a mindfulness skill that

emphasizes spontaneous participation in activities without self-consciousness. You engage in an activity without the sense of being separate from the activity that self-consciousness brings. In self-conscious activity you are one step removed because you are judging how well you are doing or how you are being viewed by others. You can be conscious or aware without being self-conscious. The mindfulness skill of participating means participating with consciousness or awareness, not daydreaming or functioning on automatic pilot in a trance. Observing and describing are preliminary steps toward dropping observing and describing so you can participate fully in life with awareness.

You are not an observer, a spectator, a commentator, or a witness to life. You are a full participant.

With awareness in the present moment, you transcend space and time. There is open spacious awareness with no inside and no outside. There is no one inside your head observing what is going on inside or outside your head. You are not the talking voice inside your head. There is no one in there who steps back to witness life as it passes you by. Seeing and responding flow seamlessly together. You don't observe, you live your precious life moment by moment. It is not you witnessing your life. It is just this life in all its freshness and fullness.

Coming face-to-face with life itself you participate with awareness and you are transformed in the process. There is no subject observing an object. The duality of observer and observed, of subject and object, is seen through completely—and seeing through is different than observing or witnessing. You simultaneously see through the observer, the observed, and any sense of separation between observer and observed. Subject and object become transparent and the distance between them collapses. The wholeness and completeness of life become apparent, and with this insight into selflessness, you see that there is nothing that you lack. With no observer, no witness, no separate self, comes fullness of life.

Sitting silent and still,
letting thoughts fall away,
not clinging,
not observing,
letting go of the story of me,
self dissolves completely.
Mountains quiver green,
sky breathes.
Lacking nothing,
everything is gained.
Abundant life!

Nonseparation

ONE MORNING on my way to work, I passed by a daycare center. I saw a little girl about two years old clinging with tiny hands to a chain link fence as she watched her mother drive away. The little girl's scream of "Mamaaaaa" pierced the gray, foggy September morning— and my heart. I felt the primal pain of separation.

As you mature and develop, you outgrow the pain you felt as a toddler separating from a parent, but pain accompanies many other separations you experience throughout life: the break-up of a romantic relationship, moving far from home, losing a job, or the death of someone close to you. The pain of separation is part of what it is to be a sensitive, caring human being.

Nonseparation, therefore, means acknowledging and feeling the pain, not trying to deny it, push it away, or separate from it. Nonseparation means not putting up walls to defend yourself from the pain of life.

The view that you are a separate self in need of defense is a major source of human suffering. One of Buddha's Four Noble Truths is that the cause of suffering is selfish clinging. As life goes on, everything changes, yet we cling to the way things were or the way we wish they were. A narrow self-centered perspective on how life should be creates suffering as the actuality of life is encountered.

Meditation is a safe place to let down the walls you have built around yourself and see that there is no separate self to defend. When the walls and boundaries collapse completely, there is no separate self, no separation at all from life itself. During meditation, when you let go of words, concepts, thoughts, stories, and opinions, you are letting go of boundaries and barriers that divide and create the illusion that a separate self exists.

When I was a first grade teacher, we had a new science program that came with a kit to encourage hands-on discovery. The kit included a huge container of buttons. Each child was given a pile of buttons and told to sort the buttons into several smaller piles. No instructions were given about how to sort the buttons. The children didn't seem to need further instructions; they eagerly went about the task of sorting their buttons. When they were finished sorting, we took a look at the piles of buttons arranged on their desks. Some of the children sorted the buttons by color, some by size, some by the material they were made of, and one child sorted according to whether the button had two holes, four holes, or a loop on the back to attach it. I was amazed by this lesson as it unfolded before my eyes. It helped me clearly see how concepts like color, size, material, and number are used to separate or divide the reality that surrounds us. The children showed me that reality can be divided in different ways, depending on what you choose to focus on.

In meditation you focus on letting go of all concepts and ideas such as self and other, mine and yours, inside and outside; when all divisions and boundaries fall away you experience firsthand nonseparation or unbounded awareness. You see that there is no separate self. You wake up from the nightmare of separation and see that you are not alone.

On a recent trip to the beach we went to an aquarium that had a tunnel of glass to walk through. You could see fish of all different colors, shapes, and sizes swimming above your head and to each side. Walking through the tunnel of fish, you could see and feel that you are not alone on this earth. Life is teeming all around you wherever you go: fish, birds, animals, trees, weeds, insects, and microbes. Seeing through the boundaries of kingdom, phylum, class, order, family, genus, and species that divide life up into categories, you are no longer cut off from life.

You don't end at your skin; you are an inseparable manifestation of the whole, changing from moment to moment. You only need to let down the barriers and boundaries you have erected to create a separate sense of self, to let down the walls and open to wholeness. It is an ongoing process of opening moment by moment. So quickly we build up walls and defenses again, and that is why regular meditation practice and attention in daily life are necessary.

It's not that concepts, words, and thoughts are not necessary for survival or useful for many purposes in the world. However, rational, linear thought tends to multiply, dominate, and crowd out other ways of knowing and being such as appreciation, intuition, wonder, awe, mystery, and not knowing. Concepts, words, and thoughts divide, cover over, and obscure the direct experience of the unity of life.

The paradox of nonseparation is that nonseparation contains separation and allows individuation to occur without obscuring the underlying unity of life. When you have the direct experience of nonseparation, of no separate self, you are freed from the fear of separation. Therefore you stop grasping and clinging onto self and others, which creates endless suffering. This frees both you and the people in your life. Nonseparation empowers you to appreciate, develop, and express your own unique gifts without being self-centered.

Buddhists sometimes use the word *emptiness* to express the experience of no separate self or unbounded awareness. What are emptied out are boundaries, and thus separation and division of the whole. Psychologists tell us that a clear sense of personal identity and personal boundaries are essential for mental health and well-being. It is true that these are necessary, but they are not sufficient. Self is not a static, fixed entity; it is an ongoing, dynamic process. Self changes and can be transformed. Boundaries are needed, but not rigid boundaries.

Meditation helps you develop flexible boundaries.

When useful, you establish clear, appropriate boundaries. When closeness and intimacy are desired, boundaries are allowed to dissolve completely. Your boundaries change fluidly as the situation requires. They are not walls made of brick and mortar.

Venkat, a graduate student from India who meditates with New River Zen Community, shared the following story with the group as we meditated together one Saturday. When he was a middle school student he enjoyed playing cricket with his classmates in the schoolyard and was quite good at it. He attended a school that was surrounded by a high wall. Occasionally the ball was hit so hard that it went over the wall and the game remained in play while one of the players climbed out over the wall to retrieve the ball.

On one such occasion, he was the one to climb out over the wall to retrieve the ball. The ball landed a short distance beyond the wall, against the side of an apartment building. As he reached to pick up the ball he looked into the window of one of the apartments. The apartment was sparsely furnished, but clean and neat with a kitchen set up in one corner of the small room. A little girl was sitting in a chair by the kitchen table as her mother combed her hair. He could see that they were poor, but not destitute. He was struck by the loving way the mother cared for her little daughter. All this flashed before him and touched him deeply as he hesitated momentarily before running back to the wall to climb over and resume the game while his teammates cheered him on.

From that day on, he thought about what it was that the walls around the school were walling in or walling out. The students were told the walls were for safety purposes, but he couldn't stop thinking of the human intimacy he had witnessed beyond the wall and feeling that his life was diminished by being separated from it and from all the life going on just beyond the walls.

Sometimes we need boundaries or walls for safety reasons, but with every gain in safety, there is a loss of intimacy with the whole of life. Boundaries are a part of life, and so we embrace appropriate boundaries and establish them skillfully, but it is crucial for us to see them for what they are, and to also be able to see beyond and through them to unbounded awareness and love.

I am the mountain.
No distance
Between me and the farthest star.

I am life
Vibrant, full, pulsating
Fragile, fleeting, precious.

NONSEPARATION

No boundaries
Divide and fragment
No boundaries in the whole universe.

Yet every leaf, each person, each form
Exquisitely individual
All its own.

Undefended, soft, open
We breathe together.
Eyes meet.

We are vast
Larger than I can say
Nothing excluded.

Face-to-face with all that is one-by-one
Bird's song is my song
Baby's cry is my cry
Pain of separation pierces to the marrow.
Nonseparation sets the spirit free.

Not the Same, Not Different

EXPERIENCING NONSEPARATION, that you are one with everything, is just the first step. Your inseparable interdependence with everything is easy to understand intellectually, and sometimes this intellectual understanding is mistaken for the direct experience of ego boundaries coming down completely to reveal the magnificent oneness of life. Some people call the experience of oneness nonduality. But this creates another duality, namely, duality versus nonduality. In Zen the expression "not one, not two" is used to embrace both the one and the many, the universal and the particular. Both realities must be appreciated and integrated as the whole of life, and must be lived out in each precious moment. This is a more complete experience of nonduality that is not limited to oneness but fully cherishes the particular as a vibrant manifestation of the whole.

The particular is distinguishable but not separate or different from the universal. This subtle distinction is conveyed in Zen with the image of a white heron standing in snow. At first glance, the white heron is well camouflaged and blends into the snowy landscape. But when you look more carefully, the pattern of the great bird standing there comes to the fore; the heron is distinguished from the drifts of bright white snow. The heron is not separate from the white world but is distinct and recognizable by its pattern and movement.

I have never seen a white heron, but once when my husband and I were leaving a retreat center in western New York, two great blue herons lifted off the pond beside the dirt road and flew ahead of us, leading the way. We were inspired by the elegance of the large birds taking flight, paired up like us, as individuals and together, unique and exquisite expressions of something vast beyond our knowing. Universal ultimate reality can be known in the particular.

Standing on a hilltop you can see the beauty all around you extending in every direction and feel a deep unity with everything. You look off to the horizon and exclaim, "It's so beautiful!" But it is a greater challenge to feel and exclaim, "I'm so beautiful!" You, like the natural beauty all around you, are the elegant functioning of the whole. Extend your arms, take a twirl, and say, "I am elegant! I am whole."

These exclamations may sound strange in a section of a book titled "Experiencing Selflessness." They may sound narcissistic, egotistical, or arrogant. But selflessness means freeing yourself from the limited view of a separate self. When you experience yourself as not separate from the whole, as instead the functioning of the whole, the limitations you place upon yourself drop away. The experience is self-liberating. Selflessness means dropping your attachment to a limited, separate self. Realizing your unity with all of life, with all people everywhere, with the whole, with God, you appreciate the gift and miracle of your unique life. In our experience of the universal, the unrepeatable beauty and value of the particular is highlighted. Each of us is a beautiful white heron standing with grace and dignity in the pure white snow.

It is the limited ego-self that sees itself as separate from everything else and therefore values itself above all else. It defends itself with thick armor and fights to the death to protect itself. This is where the fear of death enters in, as the separate ego worries about coming to an end. This is where greed enters in, as the separate ego senses its basic lack, its insubstantiality. The separate ego-self can never get enough; it is selfish rather than selfless.

Sometimes when I babysit my granddaughter, she wants to watch cartoons on television. Especially as Christmas approaches there are alluring advertisements for the latest toys that make them seem far more exciting than they actually are. With each ad, my granddaughter says, "I want that." The ads are carefully crafted to cultivate the potential for greed that resides within each of us from an early age. Fancy ads are equally effective in creating wants and needs in adults. We want the latest styles—a new kitchen with granite countertops and stainless steel appliances, designer fashions, and this year's model of car. The separate ego-self is like a hungry ghost, until finally we realize that ghosts are not real.

Meditation is about seeing the hungry ghost for what it is. Meditation is not aimed at self-improvement; the goal is not to make the limited ego-self better in some way, less self-centered or less greedy. It lifts the veil of ignorance and provides a way to see through and beyond the illusion of a separate self altogether. This is not self-transcendence, because the separate self does not exist in the first place. You see right through the separate ego-self, and when the illusion is seen for what it is, it dissipates into thin air. In its place is clear-eyed awareness of the unity of life. The particular, including your own unique circumstances and gifts, are distinguished and appreciated, but not separated or isolated.

Seeing that we are not the same and not different is especially valuable in our interactions with other people. Our common humanity is deeply felt. There is no need to deny positive or negative feelings that are aspects of being a human being. Each feeling has its own distinct qualities. During meditation you become acquainted with feelings as they first arise and see how they ebb and flow without the need to push them away or feed them. This familiarity with human emotions allows you to embrace them as a rich aspect of your humanity without the need to express or act on them in inappropriate ways. Feelings are not things. They are patterns or movements, as are you. Meditation allows you to experience the spaciousness of the whole of life that puts feelings into a broader perspective.

After a weeklong retreat, a friend and I went driving through the nearby city so she could show me the neighborhood where she grew up. Her parents had gotten divorced when she was a young girl and her childhood had been lonely and painful for her. As we drove past her old school, she pointed out the playground where she used to go to get out of the cold atmosphere of her house. She had been in therapy for many years to work through her feelings resulting from a lack of warmth and family life. She told me that during the retreat she had an experience of opening, of greater spaciousness. In this expanded experience, the pain of her childhood assumed a new perspective and consumed less of her energy. The pain was still there, and could be distinguished, but it was like a puddle within a lake. It was because of this experience that she wanted to visit her old neighborhood that day, anxious to see if the waves of emotion that depressed her whenever she visited there, and at holiday times and family gatherings, still overwhelmed her when she returned. She was greatly relieved, and joyous, to find that the emotions she usually felt were no longer tidal waves of hurt and grief, but more like the ripples caused by raindrops.

Experiencing the unity of our common humanity does not obscure our differences; it provides a space in which you can appreciate both your sameness and uniqueness. You are not compelled by the ego to make a statement and stand out from the crowd, nor do you feel compelled to conform so you don't stand out. The experience of human unity gives you the freedom to stand on your own two feet and the courage to join hands with others.

Two eyes
One nose
Two ears
One mouth
Not just one
Not just two
One face appearing
As many faces!

Human Affection

To KNOW and understand yourself, deep insight into your need for human affection is essential. To a newborn infant, human affection is as essential as food for survival, growth, and development. Human affection takes the form of touching, holding, rocking, making eye contact, smiling, and responding to the infant's crying with feeding, diapering, and comforting. Infants who don't receive love and affection may develop failure to thrive—they may not gain weight and grow normally. Infants and toddlers raised in environments lacking human warmth and affection, such as crowded orphanages or homes with negligent caregivers, are at risk for developing an attachment disorder. This adversely affects their ability to interact socially and behave appropriately.

For several years I worked as a nurse in an intensive care nursery caring for premature or ill newborns. Based on the large body of research demonstrating that infants need human affection in order to develop normally, we nurses gave great attention not only to the medical and physical needs of the infants in our care but also their needs for human interaction, touch, and love. Some of the babies were too sick to be held, so we gently stroked them, talked to them, and sang to them. When they opened their eyes, we came face-to face with them, smiled at them, and made loving eye contact. Parents were encouraged to be with their baby as much as possible, and as soon as the baby's health permitted, they were helped to hold, rock, and feed their baby. Babies' lives depend on the care and attention of loving adults.

Human affection takes many forms. In its most basic form it is the sense you get that someone likes you, that they want you around, that they enjoy your presence and delight in you. Their affection communicates to you "I'm glad you exist." In receiving human affection, you affirm your right to exist and be loved.

Once during meditation a picture flashed into my mind, a memory of me, at age two, standing in my crib in my pajamas, waving my blue blanket up and down to smooth out the wrinkles before crawling under it to go to sleep. My mother was busy in the adjacent bedroom, taking care of my brother who was fifteen months younger than me. With this image came the realization that although I could, from an early age, manage some of my own needs for care and comforting, there remained a huge need for love from others. The depth of my need for human love and affection was a revelation to me and I became sensitive to this need in myself and others. In seeing this directly, and feeling it in my bones and marrow, I connected more fully to all of humanity.

Human affection can take the form of touch and physical closeness. When I was a toddler, my father used to sit me on his lap in his big easy chair while he relaxed after a long day of work while reading *Time* or *National Geographic*. Even though he wasn't reading to me, I enjoyed looking at the pictures, and most of all, the closeness and affection of just being with him. Sometimes my granddaughter climbs up onto my lap and says, "Grandma, will you hold me?" She has the confidence to ask for what she wants and needs. I receive as much affection from holding her as she does from being held.

Human affection is expressed as much through touch and nonverbal cues as it is through words. We feel affection in a pat on the shoulder, a hug, a kiss, or holding hands as we walk together down the road. We see it in facial expressions of joy and concern. It can be conveyed in the wink of an eye. We don't just hear affection in words, but also in an animated or gentle tone of voice. We feel it in the silence of someone listening and in our being heard.

Recently a friend received a diagnosis of life-threatening cancer. He was greatly relieved to find a surgeon in whom he had confidence and in whom he sensed human caring and affection. When the surgeon sat down with him and his wife to explain his upcoming surgery, at one point in their conversation the surgeon reached out and held his hand and his wife's hand. Both he and his wife were deeply touched by this gesture and the surgeon's touch affirmed their importance to him and their shared humanity. This kind of affection and affirmation is life-giving in illness and in health.

Words also have the power to convey genuine affection. I recently visited a friend whom I had not seen for many years. Since I last saw her she had gotten divorced and remarried. It was fun to go out together and spend time getting to know her new husband. Knowing how critical her previous husband had been of her, it was particularly moving, in the midst of our dinner conversation, to hear her say with confidence, happiness, and pride regarding her new husband, "He only says nice things about me!"

The need for human affection is so great that it is good to develop a web of affection that extends all around you, in your relationship with your lover, with family, with friends, and with people in the community and organizations you belong to. No one person, no matter how wonderful, can meet all your needs. In being affectionate to others, you develop close relationships in which you receive affection. In being the love that you are, there is no limit to the amount of love you can share.

My best friend Karen moved into the house across the street when we were in fifth grade. I remember going over to meet her for the first time and being taken aback by seeing her, at the age of ten, still playing with a baby doll. I never liked dolls. Even if I were the kind of girl who did like dolls, I was sure that I would have outgrown them by ten. Despite our differences, we quickly became fast friends, going back and forth across the street many times a day to spend time together. We shared a mutual affection and enjoyed everything we did together, from horseback riding to swimming, or just talking and giggling.

But what impressed me most about Karen was that she genuinely liked all the other children at school and in the neighborhood and was kind and loving toward them. She never joined in when a child was being teased or rejected. She showed me an alternative to the usual childhood behaviors of name calling, gossiping, and separating into cliques, us against them. She was a truly affectionate and friendly person and showed me that this is possible. From her I learned that nothing is lost and everything is gained in being this way. All these many years later, Karen and I are still best friends, and although we live far apart, I can feel her love and affection across the miles.

Our need for human affection is so much a part of who we are as human beings that we sometimes find ourselves going to extremes to get this need met. For example, I have the tendency to try very hard to please people so I will be liked and appreciated. This pattern defends me against the feeling that I am lacking in some way and not deserving of love for just being the unique human being that I am. This pattern is egotistical, reinforcing the ego's need to gain approval. Recognizing this pattern for what it is, and acknowledging my need for affection as an integral part of being human, the grip of this habitual way of behaving is loosened. Seeing that I am, from the beginning, a loving human being opens me to be love and receive love. Love and affection are not earned, they are pure gift.

The Dalai Lama says, "We can live without religion and meditation, but we cannot survive without human affection." This applies literally to our survival, growth, and development as infants and children, but it is equally applicable in our lives as adults. When we give and receive human affection, we come to life. The absence of love and affection leads to depression, loneliness, dullness, lifelessness, and death. Religious beliefs without loving actions ring hollow or become divisive and aggressive when human affection is not primary. Hour after hour of meditation can turn us into stone buddhas if we don't recognize and act on the primacy of human affection and love in each small gesture and each bold stroke. Enlightenment is not an idea or state of being; it is intimacy moment by moment.

A moving example of this in the Christian tradition is the story in John 12:3–8 of Mary pouring out expensive oil to wash the feet of Jesus with her hair. When she was criticized for this extravagance and told that the oil could have been sold and the money used to help the poor, Jesus defended Mary and her act of affection and love saying that it was a fitting gesture. "You will always have the poor with you but you will not always have me." Human affection is for the particular, and takes place with wholehearted appreciation of the fleeting beauty of each person and each moment of life.

Without human affection,
we wither and die of thirst.
A whisper, a glance, a smile
refreshes like a glass of cool water.
Life flows back into us.
In the giving and in the receiving
we are the love we need.

Just as I Am

"JUST AS I AM" is the title of one of my favorite hymns. In the context of experiencing selflessness, this phrase contains both the particular "I am" and the great "I AM WHO I AM" of Exodus 3:14, ineffable and beyond name. It is from the perspective of the later "I AM" that the particular "I am" is fully accepted and appreciated. These two are not separate.

The limited, separate ego-self is critical and judgmental, wanting everyone, including you, to conform to its constricted view and standards. The separate self does not know the worth of the great I AM or value its manifestation in each person, including yourself. As discussed in previous chapters, self is not a separate, static entity; it is a changing, fluid functioning of the whole. This view of self is what is meant by "selflessness." It is a hopeful view that embraces exactly how you are in each moment, along with the awareness that there is unlimited potential for change and growth.

My cousin and his wife have a new baby, Zoe. Zoe's grandparents live far away so her dad attached a webcam to her playpen so the grandparents can watch her play via computer. Babies grow and change so fast and her grandparents did not want to miss any of her development. It is enlivening to see Zoe's fresh baby face. Her smile lights up her whole face, along with the faces of everyone who sees her. She is inquisitive, handling and inspecting her toys thoroughly, to figure out how they work. When trying to walk, if she falls down, she isn't discouraged; she gets right back up again. She is persistent and has confidence in herself, just as she is. There is a saying that babies are straight from heaven. This is because it's easy to see the great I AM manifesting in their freshness, spontaneity, and liveliness. We accept and appreciate babies and young children just as they are, even when they are cranky and it is clearly naptime.

It's more difficult to accept and appreciate adults, especially yourself. The first time my granddaughter heard the song "Jesus Loves the Little Children," she asked me, "Does He love adults too?" I answered, "Yes, He loves adults too." This is our challenge, to love adults too, in all their complexity, just as they are.

Although much is written about self-acceptance, there is a need to move beyond both the sense of a separate self and acceptance of the separate self, to move beyond the dualities of self and other and of accepting or rejecting. The word *appreciation* seems more appropriate than the word *acceptance*. Appreciation includes not just accepting but also valuing, cherishing, and treasuring yourself and your life. In experiencing the particular as not separate from the great "I AM," there comes the welling up of great waves of appreciation, gratitude, and praise.

Appreciating yourself just as you are, you do not try to push away or deny your limitations, conditioning, blind spots, or shadows. This is one of the greatest values of an ongoing meditation practice. By taking the time to stop and sit quietly each day, attentive and alert, you gradually become more aware of subtle aspects of yourself. In the light of awareness, some of your harmful conditioning and blind spots dissolve; some don't. Being aware of the negative patterns that remain, you gain compassion and empathy for yourself and others because you realize there is no way to know and eliminate all of your conditioning and shadows. There are issues that remain unresolved. Part of appreciating yourself just as you are is an appreciation for that which is unresolved.

Appreciating yourself, just as you are, also frees you from the heavy burden of perfectionism. Some of us are hardest on ourselves, expecting perfection. Others expect perfection from others or from life in general. Perfection of ourselves, others, or life is an unrealistic expectation that creates tremendous tension and suffering. The antidote is appreciation. This means simply seeing that everything is just as it is and not as you or anyone else thinks it should be. You experience the peace and spaciousness of everything just as it is. Imperfection is part of the texture and richness of life. It has a beauty, truth, and goodness all its own.

My husband and I lived out on the Navajo reservation in

the late sixties and early seventies. At that time there were still many traditional Navajos in the area who made their living by herding sheep and weaving rugs and baskets. We were invited to attend many ceremonies. In Navajo ceremonies the rituals, songs, dances, and prayers are not aimed at asking for things such as a cure for an illness or trying to control things such as the rain. The ceremonies mainly focus on *hozho*, bringing the people back into balance and harmony with the community, the earth, and the whole. The Navajo sing of walking in beauty, which means living in harmony with the whole, just as it is.

There is a Zen poem titled "Trust in Mind." It is a poem about how picking and choosing according to your likes and dislikes diminishes life and makes it more difficult. Picking life apart causes it to lose its unity, wholeness, and fullness. "Trust in mind" refers to the wholeness of life just as it is. Trust allows you to appreciate yourself just as you are and your life just as it is.

My ninety-two-year-old friend tells me she's had a full life, with a wonderful husband and son, a successful career, and after retirement time for travel and friends. But now she feels weak and shaky, unable to do most of the things she used to enjoy like bicycle riding, dancing, and gardening. She says she is ready to die and that she doesn't fear death. She says, "I trust that whatever the Lord has in mind for me after I die is okay with me." This attitude of trust is as applicable to life before death as it is to life after death. It is trust in what is larger than our small capacity to pick and choose.

The danger associated with picking and choosing is highlighted in Matthew 13:29 in the parable of the wheat and the weeds. The wheat stands for the good in the world and the weeds represent the evil. In the fields, the wheat and the weeds grow mixed in together, and the servants are cautioned to leave the weeds alone, lest they accidentally uproot the wheat as well. The story cautions us about thinking that we can sort the good from the bad and make ourselves or our world perfect. It suggests that a broader vision than our own is necessary since there is so much that we do not know.

In Matthew 7:1 we are warned, "Do not judge, so that you may not be judged." When you judge others and the value of life itself, you will find that you develop the habit of judging. This habit extends to judging everything, including yourself. An open, nonjudgmental attitude is kinder toward both yourself and others. A nonjudgmental attitude liberates both self and others. However, we do like some things and dislike others, and we do have to make many judgments and choices every day. Yet at the same time, we can avoid falling into the trap of being judgmental and act with the awareness of how our likes and dislikes, our picking and choosing, block a broader vision and joy in life.

In Zen, the world of things, thoughts, and feelings is called "the world of form." The ineffable, infinite, ultimate reality is called "formlessness" or "emptiness." When form and formless are experienced as one and the same, there is a freshness and intimacy with life itself that is called nonduality or "just this." When there is no gap at all between you and your life moment by moment, no gap between you and God, then you not only accept yourself, just as you are, and your life, just as it is; you experience life with appreciation, wonder, trust, and love.

No imitation

Unique

Without comparison

One hundred percent you

Just as you are

Just this

Breathing

Walking

Sitting

Laughing

Crying

Singing

Dancing

Eating

Sleeping

Awakening!

Opening to God

Who Loves

OUR LIVES are constrained because we have a limited view of who we are and who God is. We are living restrictedly.

These two fundamental spiritual questions—"Who am I?" and "Who is God?"—are linked. In our discussion of selflessness we have been dealing with the first question, but it is by looking deeply into the second that we address the question of "Who am I?" more fully.

This is not an intellectual exercise. You are not searching for theological or philosophical answers to these questions. The intuitive process of questioning, of deeply penetrating inquiry, is itself how we encounter the "who" of both these questions.

Meditation, as presented in this book, is a process of releasing. During meditation you let go of thoughts, concepts, beliefs, and opinions about yourself and God; this is sometimes called *emptying*. There is a Zen saying: "When everything is utterly emptied out, there is something that cannot be emptied." To learn what it is that cannot be emptied out you must let go of every object, thought, and story about yourself and God.

In the Christian tradition this emptying process is called *kenosis*. Phillipians 2:7 speaks of Christ emptying himself and of Christians being called to follow his example. It is in emptying yourself that God's love is revealed and can be shared with others.

Letting go or emptying during meditation can also be understood from the perspective of the apophatic contemplative tradition in Christianity that says God's presence becomes clearer to us when we let go of what God is not. In the Hindu tradition the expression "Neti, neti" or "Not this, not this" exemplifies an approach of negation through which God, who is ineffable, is experienced beyond all thoughts and words. Stephen Mitchell's translation of the *Tao Te Ching* begins by saying, "The tao that can be told is not the eternal Tao." You must set aside some time to experience what it is that cannot be told. It is a refined, subtle reality you need to taste and savor for yourself.

This experience comes in as many varieties and flavors as there are individuals; some are intense and some are more subtle. One woman on a recent retreat was meditating, paying attention to her breathing, when she had such an experience. She told me afterward, "I just opened up. I had no idea!" She said she had been alternately laughing and crying all day because it was so beautiful. "I'm so open. I'm so alive. I'm not separate from anything. It's so joyous. This morning during breakfast I couldn't stop laughing. During walking meditation I was laughing, and it seemed as if the leaves rustling in the breeze, and the gravel crunching under my feet, were laughing too. Then later I saw everyone sitting in meditation and each and every one of them was so beautiful. I started crying because I could see that there is nothing but God's love everywhere. I *am* God's love everywhere. Why couldn't I see this all along?"

Another woman came to see me who was serene and peaceful. She said that when the meditation bell rang, she rang, and continued ringing right out to the ends of the universe. In that ringing her whole world shifted and reverberated. She said, "Everything was ringing. The hills and hedgerows were ringing. I was ringing with no boundaries or obstructions. It was the ringing of freedom and love that could not be stopped since there were no barriers anywhere. There are no words to describe it. I'm free and open to life and love, to *be* love." Then she became silent, just sitting, breathing, and ringing.

These are not experiences that the self has. These are experiences that transform the way self is experienced. You see that your small separate self does not exist; it is a misperception. You are vast—and you and God are not separate realities.

The Buddhist narrative is that you are not your small separate self. Suffering is caused by selfish clinging to the limited ego-self. The way out of suffering is the Eightfold Path, which includes meditation. Wisdom is letting go of the separate self and experiencing that you are vast and boundless. You are a manifestation of ultimate reality, as is everything you see. Ultimate reality is beyond words so Buddhists will say nothing about it, although at times, they may refer to it as "not knowing." In this ineffable, expanded experience of reality, compassion arises as you see and feel that you are not separate from others.

The Christian narrative is that there is a loving God who cares about each and every one of us. From the Christian perspective, God is the ultimate reality; God is love. In Jesus, God took human form, to show us the path of love on earth. Jesus, who is one with God, urges us to experience this unity and see that we, too, are love. We are challenged to live out this reality by loving one another, especially those most in need.

These two different views are complementary. The strength of Buddhism is its well-developed methods of meditation, which expand our vision till we experience our identity with ultimate reality. The word *identity* here refers to the insight that you and ultimate reality are not two separate realities, which can come together and unite. You realize your true identity; from the beginning you are a manifestation of ultimate reality. The strength of Christianity is the experience of God's love, a love that humanizes, heals, frees, transforms, and unites us. Both traditions lead to compassionate action, and each has the power to reinforce the other in meeting the tremendous need for love, compassion, and healing in our world.

Many Christians benefit from the regular practice of Buddhist meditation, which carries them beyond their usual prayer forms that rely on words and concepts. As a result they are able to move beyond the duality of a relationship with God to the nondual experience of identity with God. Identity with God is not foreign to Christianity; it is included in passages such as John 10:30, when Jesus says, "I and my Father are one." In Galatians 2:20, Saint Paul says that he himself no longer lives "but Christ lives in me . . ." The experience of identity with God and with God's love is brought into the foreground by meditation practice.

Christianity brings to the fore a God who cares and loves. Sometimes Buddhists too speak in more personal ways about ultimate reality. In *The Record of Transmitting the Light* Zen Master Dongshan composed the following verse after he looked into a stream, saw his face reflected there in the water, and was awakened.

> Avoid seeking Him in someone else
> Or you will be far apart from the Self.
> Solitary now am I, and independent,
> But I meet Him everywhere.
> He surely is me,
> But I am not Him.
> Understanding it in this way,
> You will be directly one with thusness.

This verse clarifies what is meant by *identity*. "He surely is me" refers to Master Dongshan's realization that he is a manifestation of God. "But I am not Him" refers to his realization that he is not the totality of God, and although he can experience God's presence, more of God remains that he, as a human being, doesn't have the capacity to know.

In *The Art of Just Sitting*, John Daido Loori offers a beautiful Zen verse that conveys great caring:

On the tips of ten thousand grasses
each and every dewdrop contains the light of
the moon.
Since the beginning of time,
not a single droplet has been forgotten.
Although this is so,
some may realize it and some may not.

When you realize, even to a small extent, that "not a single droplet has been forgotten," new life is breathed into you and you are able to love more fully. This verse is similar to Jesus saying in Luke 12:6, "Are not five sparrows sold for two pennies? Yet not one of them is forgotten in God's sight." It is important for each one of us to know that our life matters. You, like a single droplet or a sparrow, are not forgotten. You are cared for and loved.

"Who loves" is both a question and a response. You and God are not two separate realities. God loves. You love. God's love and your love are one reality.

Wind rustles the leaves, but who can see it?
You can't pick it up in your hand.
You can't grab hold of the sky.
You can't describe it with words.
You can't take a picture of it.
But if you are very quiet for a long time
or when you least expect it
in the blink of an eye
you disappear
and who is here:
the wind, the earth, the sky,
and your breathing.

Who Loves Who(m)

WHEN YOU SURRENDER your small, limited view of self and of God—letting go of all your thoughts about God to experience the breadth and depth of vast, infinite reality, unmediated by thoughts and words, no matter how sublime—you see that it is not you who loves. It is God who loves. Another way to say this is that God loves through you. You are the functioning of God's love. You are an expression of God's love. This insight is liberating because your love as a small, separate self is limited, whereas God's love flows freely. It is abundant and unlimited. It is the living water needed to sustain life.

Saint Augustine used the phrase "one Christ loving himself." Since Christ and God are one, rather than two gods, this idea can be applied to say that there is one God loving himself. In the unity of God and each person, "God loves God." But on an intellectual level alone, this understanding is not liberating. You need to experience it for yourself.

Sitting silently in meditation with the body alert and the mind alert, you let go of all thoughts, feelings, and ideas, awake and aware in the present. When the cloud of your mental chatter disperses, you no longer sit in a fog. You see clearly. You see that your eyes are God's eyes. You see yourself, everyone, and everything through God's eyes. God's eyes are the eyes of love and compassion. Seeing clearly is a moment-by-moment ongoing process. It is open ended. You keep opening the eyes of your heart to see anew each moment.

In the *Gateless Gate* Zen Master En says, "Even Shakyamuni and Maitreya are servants of that one. Just tell me, who is that one?" In other words, both the historical Buddha and the buddha of the future are servants of that one; throughout time and space buddhas serve that one. Not only the great buddhas, but you and I as well, serve that one. Who is that one?

This question urges you to inquire deeply and see into this matter for yourself, not with your intellect alone, but with your intuition, your whole heart, and every cell in your body. What you will see is that the one who serves, the one who is served, and the serving itself are one. The one who loves, the one who is loved, and the loving itself are one. Who loves who. In proper English one would say "Who loves whom." However, this implies a duality of subject and object, so "Who loves who" is more correct. This isn't an answer to the question, "Who is that one?" because the answer lies far beyond words and phrases. The answer transcends space and time, and yet it is immanent right here and now, warm and breathing.

God is not found in thoughts and words but in this

breathing, pulsating reality in which you live and move. You are the mountains, lakes, and rivers. You are the towering oak tree glistening green in the sunlight. You are the great ocean, the waves, and all the swimming fish. You are the people everywhere working, eating, loving, and playing. You, like all things, are not a thing. You, like God, are not a thing. You are not separate from the whole swirling universe. You are not separate from God or God's love.

God's love is vast and ineffable. Yet, with humility, it can manifest in you. The small, separate self is seen through. It becomes transparent so God's infinite love shines through, unobstructed. In compassion, you extend its radiance and vitality to others, breathing new life into them. Jesus told his disciples in John 15:12 to "Love one another as I have loved you." This tells you how you are to love others—you share the love you yourself are, God's love. In loving, you become what you are.

During the years my husband and I lived on the Navajo reservation, we often visited the nearby Hopi reservation where a Hopi elder named David Monongye lived. David invited us to many ceremonies that took place in the village plaza or down in the kiva, and we were blessed to be present with him and listen to his stories about the Hopi way. After many wonderful visits he kindly explained to us that the Hopi way is only for those born into the tribe. He told us to take what we had learned from him and return to our own tradition. He said that our task was to find what was deep and meaningful in our own tradition and bring it forth to help humanity and the earth in its struggle to survive.

We returned to the tradition of our birth, Christianity. We went deeply into the tradition to discern the best it has to offer, both experientially and through study. For me, I found the essence of Christianity is to experience and share God's love.

What I found lacking in this tradition was a clear and effective method of meditation, or contemplative prayer, to experience unity with God and embody God's love in the world. I am not alone in this; people from a variety of different religious traditions have turned to Eastern meditation practices to complement their traditional prayer forms. I found that Zen meditation met my need for a spiritual practice that was deep and effective in cutting through the layers and layers of thoughts and ideas that kept me living in my head, obscuring rather than revealing the reality of God and God's love.

Along the way, I met my Zen teacher, Roshi Robert Jinsen Kennedy. He is a Jesuit priest, a Zen master, a theologian, and a psychoanalyst. For me this was the perfect combination to satisfy my seeking; in him I found the integration of Christianity, Zen, and humanity at its best. As a successor in his branch of the White Plum lineage of Zen, I follow in his footsteps and attempt to bring forward the best that these traditions have to offer and forge a path for their seamless integration.

Some people practice Zen in order to experience Buddhist emptiness. Emptiness is experienced when you let go of all thoughts, concepts, images, and boundaries. In *The Book of Equanimity*, Emperor Wu asks the great master Bodhidharma, "What is the ultimate meaning of the holy truth of Buddhism?" Bodhidharma replies, "Vast emptiness. No holiness." When you experience this for yourself, you see that emptiness is not a nihilistic void. It is the fullness of life brimming over.

I didn't begin Zen practice to experience nothingness; I wanted to experience God more intimately. By emptying out thoughts, concepts, images, and the sense of a separate self, I have been able to open to God in ways beyond what I had imagined or hoped for.

The process of emptying is expressed by Zen Master Sozan's analogy in *The Book of Equanimity* of a donkey seeing a well: the donkey sees the well, but also the well sees the donkey. "The donkey seeing the well" refers to perceiving that you are not separate from God. This experience of nonseparation allows you to see yourself through God's eyes—the well also sees the donkey. This gives rise to a great tenderness. You see yourself through the eyes of love. When you are empty of all thoughts, concepts, and boundaries, you perceive that you are not separate from God or God's love. Who loves who.

The following is a Zen story from my life experience titled "Who Rocks Who?" One day a grandmother was rocking her granddaughter in the rocking chair out on the front porch. A person passing by saw them and asked, "Is Grandma rocking the baby or is the baby rocking Grandma?" I said, "Love is rocking."

Absolute
Emptiness
Delicate, pure
Nothing

Total presence
Manifesting in the relative
Beyond symbol or meaning
Clear, bright
Love

Beyond Images

God is beyond all images because God is greater than anything a human being can imagine.

From the standpoint of the Judeo-Christian tradition, humans were created in God's image. However, typical Judeo-Christian language and imagery of God as a father make it look more like humans created God in their own image; God ends up looking, speaking, and acting like an enhanced human being. It is this anthropomorphic image of God as an all-powerful human-like figure up in heaven that leaves people struggling with religion in a scientific and postmodern era. As a result, many are moving beyond this concrete image of God. This step is a start in a positive direction, but I suggest that we need to go further, to go beyond all images of God.

On the other hand, most people find holy icons inspiring or comforting. The image makes the divine more specific and understandable. The depiction may be one such as Michelangelo's Creator, or it may be Jesus, Krishna, Shiva, or a Buddhist deity. It may be in the form of pictures, statues, or verbal descriptions. Sometimes images are used to help you realize and embody the spiritual qualities of the deity. I am not suggesting doing away with all images, but it is essential to realize their limits.

It's all too easy to find ourselves worshiping our own mental projections of God. We choose images of the divine that reinforce our human fears, trapping us in the obsessive repetition of prayers and rituals to placate an angry God who is the projection of our own fear, anger, and inability to let go of past hurts. Prayer, ritual, and even meditation can turn into pious attempts to accumulate merit as if truth, freedom, and goodness could be earned or purchased.

Images separate rather than unite. They are dualistic. For example the image of being a child of God conveys a comforting sense of security and love, but it also reinforces immaturity, which is contradictory to the Christian call to be Christ in the world. In spiritual maturity you are responsible for what you do; as it says in Matthew 25:40, "Just as you did it to one of the least of these who are members of my family, you did it to me." In this there is a step forward into maturity, responsibility, and identity. From the duality of a parent-child relationship you grow into the nonduality of seeing Christ in each person and the responsibility to be Christ through your loving response to those in need, seeing everyone as one family. Imagining God is not deep enough. You need to see that you are not separate from God and others and respond accordingly.

The previous section of this book discussed the experience of selflessness. Part of experiencing selflessness is becoming aware of your self-image and its limitation in expressing who you are as a complex, continuously changing confluence of many different factors. Each of us has many faces in different circumstances. Some situations call for a welcoming smile and others require a stern countenance. In seeing that the self is not a separate, fixed entity, the many different masks you wear are seen for what they are—images you project to accommodate various roles in life. The point is getting to know, intimately, that which is behind the mask. When all images of yourself become transparent, you see through all images of God.

There is a well-known Zen question that asks, "What was your original face before you were born?" In recent years, ultrasound images of babies taken during pregnancy have become so sophisticated that the face of your future child can be clearly seen long before the baby is born and saved for the baby book or shared online. However, this is not what this Zen question is getting at. In fact, sometimes it is stated as "What was your original face before your mother and father were born?" In many Asian countries, the idea of "saving face" is a major cultural concern. The individual does not want to bring shame to him or herself or to the family. Great effort is made to preserve one's self-image. This Zen question is asking you to look beyond your self-image to ask, "Who is the self?" The original self is your true identity, and it can never be shamed. The question urges you to experience the original self beyond any images.

Experiencing your original self, going beyond forms, requires silent, wordless meditation. Often we think of "forms" as objects in the world such as chairs, cars, dogs, or trees, but thoughts, words, concepts, feelings, and images are also forms. Meditation is not only silent, wordless prayer but also imageless prayer that allows you to experience that which is beyond form, that which is formless—to experience that you are not separate from the one formless God. The formless manifests in form; ultimately there is no separation between form and formless, between the one and the many. However, you must see beyond all forms or images, to see this for yourself.

Once I was giving a workshop on Zen meditation and after instructing the group in how to meditate, a woman raised her hand and asked, "Do you have some music you could play in the background while we meditate? It helps me calm down and feel peaceful." I explained that although music is often played in the background during relaxation exercises or guided imagery, Zen meditation is intentionally done in silence. This is because music is a form of imagery. It paints a picture with sound. Music evokes feelings and images, whereas in meditation, you are going beyond all images, no matter how soothing or uplifting they may be. You don't try to generate images, and if images come into your mind during meditation, you let them go, just as you let go of thoughts. You return your attention to your breathing. Keep it very simple.

Meditation is a way to dissolve all images of self and God that obscure your vision. However, outside of meditation it can be helpful to use images, such as the image of the sky in the following verse from Master Keizan in *The Record of Transmitting the Light*:

> If you want to reveal the sky, do not cover it up.
> It is empty, tranquil, and originally bright.

God is formless, clear, and bright like the sky. Don't cover God over with images, theories, or theologies. Don't hide God behind the mask of false images. Don't hide yourself behind it either. You are formless, clear, and originally bright like the sky.

Even subtle, sublime images obscure rather than reveal God's face. To hold in your mind the image of a loving God, for example, is saying too much since there are many meanings for the word *love* and many meanings for the word *god*. You get lost in words and meanings and lose touch with the reality they represent. Love is not an image or concept. It can't be contained by a word. Loving is not an adjective, it is a verb. A loving God is not found in an image; loving is found in the doing and God's image is seen in every face you encounter. This includes the face you see in the mirror each morning.

Beyond form and formless
Beyond being and non-being
Beyond silence and song
Free of all images
Love's light in your eyes
No picture can capture
Your wild, natural beauty

Unknowable and Ineffable

GOD IS UNKNOWABLE and ineffable. We can't know
God through the intellect or grasp God mentally.
God is beyond empirical knowledge, whether gained
through the senses or through their technological exten-
sion: telescopes, microscopes, laboratory equipment, and
computers. The magnificence of scientific knowledge, and
the intricacy of all that we know about the world, speaks
to many people of something that is beyond the material, but we cannot know God through measurement and
reasoning.

God is beyond words, concepts, and ideas—so we can't
use them to describe or explain God. Words, concepts,
and ideas divide the world into categories and do not
allow us to speak of the whole all at once. God cannot be
divided or reduced into discrete parts. Besides, we cannot
put into words what we cannot know.

Although you cannot know God with thought and
intellect, you can have an intuitive experience of God's
presence. In meditation you pay attention with all your
senses open, but you do not intentionally engage in
thinking. In this silent, attentive space, you experience

without naming or thinking about what you perceive. Open, aware, beyond words and directed thought, you become intimate with life just as it is, moment by moment. Being awake and aware in the present moment generates a sense of awe and wonder as you come face-to-face with what is. You see everyday reality as extraordinary, as the functioning of ultimate reality, God, or the unknowable whole.

God is encountered in intimacy with the whole of life, intimacy with what is. In intimacy you move beyond a mere relationship with a God who is seen as being apart from yourself to experiencing nonseparation. In the stillness and silence of meditation, you experience God's presence in subtler and subtler ways. God is infinitely subtle so there are always further insights, there is always more to be seen. This is why the Heart Sutra ends by urging us to always keep going: "Going, going, going on beyond, fully beyond, awaken, rejoice!"

When you are awake and aware, you experience God everywhere throughout your daily life. Saint Paul says in Acts 17:28, "In him we live and move and have our being." With awareness, every movement, every gesture, every small act is God's movement or functioning. When you wash the dishes, you encounter God in the bubbles, the warm water, the scrubbing, and the rinsing. There is no need for the word or idea of God—bubbles, water, scrubbing, and rinsing are enough. When you look out your window across the lawn, God sparkles like a jewel in the form of a dewdrop on each blade of grass. Do not let the word or idea of God separate you from the sparkling. God sparkles, you sparkle, just this sparkling.

As Saint Paul points out, our being is in God's being. Our being and God's being are not separate. Intimacy with God is not found in what we think or know about God but rather in our being and doing. Each act of love such as driving a sick neighbor to a doctor's appointment is an opportunity to be God's love in the world. When you act in a loving way, you become a loving human being. In this alignment of your actions and being with God's being you experience God in your life. Although you can't know God intellectually, God manifests through your actions and being.

Not knowing is an important aspect of spirituality. God always remains an unknowable mystery. The following Zen verse from *The Record of Transmitting the Light* illustrates this sense of not knowing.

> Moonlight reflected in the bottom of the pond
>   is bright in the sky;
> The water reaching up to the sky is totally clear
>   and pure.
> Though you scoop it up repeatedly and try to know it,
> Vast, clarifying all, it remains unknown.

In this verse, the moonlight represents ultimate reality, the absolute, or God—at once shining in the sky and penetrating all the way to the bottom of the pond. The water represents the relative or phenomenal world, which contains and reflects the moonlight. The pond is in the moonlight and moonlight is in the pond. Although God can be seen clearly reflected in the relative world, God cannot be held on to with your hands or grasped with your mind no matter how hard you try. The moonlight is insubstantial. The water, like life itself, is fluid, constantly changing shape so it slips through your fingers if you try to hold on to it. Although God can be seen manifesting in the relative, God remains ungraspable and unknown.

Not knowing is not the opposite of knowing. Not knowing is not ignorance. Ignorance is thinking you know when you don't. Ignorance is the arrogance of false certainty; it is holding fast to your constricting opinions and judgments. Not knowing is opening to the whole of life, what you agree with and what you disagree with, your truth and the truths of others. It is being open to others who have different experiences and perspectives than your own. Not knowing is appreciating how God manifests in other people and listening to them without judging them. In listening without judging, you come to know others, and at the same time you experience not knowing in the realization that you can never completely know another's subjective reality.

God is experienced in life itself. Life is not so much a spiritual journey as it is a courageous adventure. On an adventure, you can expect that you will face challenges and hardships at times, but you don't hunker down in doubt, fear, and sadness. You don't deny these feelings; you face them with courage. An adventurer has an attitude of great courage and ventures off into unknown territory. The challenge is to have no fixed idea of God or spirituality, to directly encounter life, moment by moment, always moving onward, not getting stuck anywhere along the way.

Some people use various types of meditation to feel centered and grounded, but the experience of encountering life directly, moment by moment, is beyond center, and it is as groundless as it is grounded. Life as a courageous adventure is life free from the bonds of needing to feel secure and grounded. There is a Zen question that asks, "How do you step off the top of a hundred-foot pole?" This question helps you inquire into the experience of groundlessness; it asks how you step forward into life, into any new situation that arises. In reality you never know what lies ahead in life. This question brings you face-to-face with this fact. You don't deny the reality of not knowing; you just keep moving straight on into life. Life itself will uphold you even if you fall down. Get back up and keep going.

A similar idea is expressed in Matthew 8:20 when Jesus tells those wishing to follow him that "Foxes have holes, and birds of the air have nests; but the Son of Man has nowhere to lay his head." This is not meant to encourage recklessness or an irresponsible lack of planning. It is presenting the reality that the spiritual life is lived out moment by moment, responding to the needs of those you meet along the way, in touch with not knowing what will come your way in life. You can't control life even if you try. Instead you move forward, loving your life, just as it is, embracing the groundlessness and freedom of not knowing.

·····

What you cannot know—a great mystery.
Life without mystery is cold and hollow.
Everywhere mystery.
In birth,
the first breath.
In death,
the last breath.
Mystery remains.

Secular Meditation
versus Spiritual Meditation

L ATELY meditation has become increasingly popular
in the West, and it is often adopted in a secular fash-
ion that divorces it from its religious roots.

For instance, in recent decades there has been a huge
volume of research conducted regarding the effects of
meditation on the brain. In many of the studies, the meditation practice used in the research project is described as
secular. Sometimes the researcher acknowledges the Buddhist origins of a meditation practice such as mindfulness
but emphasizes that religious beliefs are not involved in
the practice and thus it is compatible with any religious
belief the study participant may hold. This is often necessary to gain entry and credibility in the universities and
medical centers where the studies are conducted, or in
order to obtain funding for the research project. The question arises regarding whether or not meditation retains its
effectiveness, power, and potential when taken out of the
context of a particular religious tradition.

To some extent, this depends on what is meant by
the effectiveness of the meditation practice. Much of

the research has focused on the use of meditation for stress management or to treat various problems such as high blood pressure, pain, anxiety, and depression. Using sophisticated neuroimaging technologies, neuroscientists are mapping out the effects of meditation on brain function and structure. Psychologists are studying the effects of meditation on attention, decision-making, and performance. The physiological and psychological effects of meditation can be measured and verified using traditional scientific methods. However, this does not account for the spiritual effects of meditation. The full power and potential of meditation to enhance the totality of our lives cannot be elucidated while ignoring spirituality, which is an integral aspect of meditation and of our lives as human beings.

Throughout my thirty-year career as a nurse, there has been an emphasis in nursing education and in clinical practice on providing holistic care for patients and their families. Holistic care includes not only providing competent physical care but also attending to the psychological, social, cultural, and spiritual needs of patients. Ironically, I experienced that psychiatric settings lagged behind medical settings in acknowledging and addressing the spiritual needs of patients. This stemmed in part from Freud's negative views of religion and his tremendous influence on the psychiatric profession. Spirituality was not a part of behavioral theory either, which was the other major influence on the profession at the time. Alcoholics Anonymous groups were the only places God or spirituality was mentioned at the hospital. This has changed gradually over the years and spirituality is now included in psychiatric care. Many psychiatric units have spirituality group meetings, and some new forms of psychotherapy such as Acceptance and Commitment Therapy emphasize the importance of spirituality. Having come this far in integrating spirituality into health care, it is unfortunate, in the name of being scientific, to regress back to denying spirituality as an important facet of the meditation practices used to treat a wide variety of physical and mental health problems.

Growing up as a child in the fifties, under the cloud of the Cold War, I was acutely aware of the ban on all forms of religion and spirituality behind the Iron Curtain. I was and am extremely grateful for the religious freedom that we enjoy in the United States. The principle of separation of church and state, however, is one reason why meditation is often presented as secular when conducting research in public institutions or when seeking funding from government agencies. However, it is also important to acknowledge and maintain the spiritual integrity of the various types of meditation being studied. A meditation practice can be viewed as spiritual without being associated with or promoting any particular religious organization. The approach to meditation discussed in this book, for instance, is best described as a spiritual practice. Although it originated in the Zen tradition, it can complement the prayer life of people from many different religious traditions or it can enhance the spiritual life of people without any religious affiliation.

Some people practice Zen meditation as Buddhists; others do not and are drawn to Buddhism more as a philosophy or a psychology. In a *New York Times* article, David Brooks coined the term "Neural Buddhists" as a name for many in the latter group. This term refers to the explosion of interest and research in the fields of psychology and the neurosciences regarding Buddhist meditation and principles. This new knowledge is bringing about significant cultural change here and abroad. Brooks identifies four key elements of this new viewpoint. "First, that the self is not a fixed entity but a dynamic process of relationships. Second, underneath the patina of different religions, people around the world have common moral intuitions. Third, people are equipped to experience the sacred, to have moments of elevated experience when they transcend boundaries and overflow with love. Fourth, God can best be conceived as the nature one experiences at those moments, the unknowable total of all there is." People with these views do not call themselves "Neural Buddhist," but these four ideas are rapidly gaining adherents. For those who would call "Neural Buddhists" secular, it is interesting to note that the experience of God is included in this list.

Although it is often said that Buddhists do not use the word God, the truth is that in many instances they do. Zen

Master Jiyu Kennett gives us fair warning that there is a spiritual or religious aspect to Zen meditation; in *Essential Zen* she says, "If you're afraid of being grabbed by God, don't look at a wall. Definitely don't sit still." Discussing in her book *Nothing Special* the stage of meditation practice where you are no longer occupied by thinking and you are able to just experience and be, Zen Master Joko Beck says, "This nonstate is what makes our practice religious. Experiencing is the realm of no time, no space, true nature. Just is-ness, thus-ness, God." She considers Zen meditation religious because the self is surrendered to what is, and the practice is not primarily for personal gain.

Meditation is primarily a practice that promotes spiritual development, allowing you to move beyond your limited separate self, beyond ego boundaries, to experience your unity with God, others, the earth, and all beings. You touch life directly, delight in it, and embrace it just as it is.

One day in a graduate nursing class that I teach, we were discussing spirituality in health care. A graduate student in the class said that when she was an undergraduate student, she wasn't interested in spirituality. But now after working as a nurse for three years in a neonatal intensive care unit she said, "I've watched babies take their first breath and taken care of babies as they took their last breath, and now I am a spiritual person."

There is nothing overtly spiritual about sitting quietly, awake and aware, paying attention to your breathing. But if you undertake this practice on a regular basis, sitting every day, it is likely that you will realize that meditation is a spiritual practice and that you have become a spiritual person.

All life sacred.
Each breath spirit.
Here where you sit,
holy ground.
Silent prayer,
opening to God.
Complete. Whole.

Loving Presence

MEDITATION IS A WAY to learn the fine art of being present.

Regular meditation practice establishes the pattern of taking a break each day from your busy life, of shifting from "doing mode" into "being mode" for a while. Letting go of thoughts, and just paying attention to breathing or the sitting itself, frees your mind of distraction. The body and mind settle. In this calm state of alert awareness, you inhabit your body and your life right here and now. No longer absent, preoccupied, or lost in your head, you are calm and fully present in the moment. This may be experienced briefly or for more extended periods of time—it may be faint or clear—but regardless, the felt quality of presence is what draws people back to meditation again and again.

What is presence? Whose presence is it? Presence is not a thing, yet it can be experienced as a moment-by-moment reality. It can't be described or grasped on to, but when you make time and space for it, you see that it has been here all along. You have been too busy thinking and doing to notice.

The limited separate ego talks incessantly about itself, about what others should or shouldn't be doing, and about how the world should or shouldn't be. This leads to more thinking and planning for improving the self, fixing others, or solving the problems of the world. The ego serves a purpose in life, but it has the tendency to take over. When you take time to see it for what it is and give it a rest for a while, you see through it completely and it no longer obscures your vision of a larger reality. Presence is that larger reality.

It is not the presence of a separate self. It is undivided presence. Your presence is not separate from God's presence. There is one presence throughout space and time.

Presence enlivens your heart. It is refreshing and rejuvenating. When you are fully present with others, they can feel it. It speaks to their hearts. There is a loving quality to presence. It connects and unites us. Loving presence heals and brings wholeness and vitality to life.

In the Zen tradition, the phrase "a boundless field of benefaction" is sometimes used to point us toward the experience of loving presence. Presence is free of boundaries. It is infinite and undivided. A boundless field is like land that is wild and free, extending off to the horizon in every direction without fences marring its natural beauty or defining its edges. Without fences it is not divided up into "mine" and "yours." Humans and animals can all roam freely. The word *benefaction* connotes that the boundless field is there for the good of everyone. Presence is boundless goodness and love.

In recent years there has been a trend to include meditation and mindfulness skills in training programs for psychotherapists. The value of these practices is that they help therapists enhance and refine their abilities to be fully present with clients during therapy. Presence is an essential element of the therapeutic relationship; it allows clients to feel truly heard by another human being. Presence connects therapists and clients with their own humanity and with the humanity of others. Loving presence is large enough and open enough to face the truth of whatever emerges in therapy and in life, without turning away. Giving your full attention is an act of love. Zen Master Ama Samy, in an article titled "Meditation and Therapy," emphasizes that meditation and psychotherapy are distinct and are for different purposes, but they also share some similarities: "For it is love that really heals and liberates, whether in meditation or in therapy." Loving presence is key in healing the mind and liberating the human spirit.

In his book *Embodied Enquiry*, psychotherapist Les Todres describes psychological development as becoming more flexible in your response to complex situations arising in life. He contends that, additionally, spiritual development goes beyond the psychological development of a more flexible self to the realization of no-self, the emptiness of your sense of a separate self. Psychological insight and spiritual insight are integrated and lived out by "enacting the unity of emptiness and love—groundless context and this careful moment." In Buddhist terms, *presence* is called "emptiness" because it is not a thing; it is empty of all things. Empty, formless presence takes form in love, in each careful moment of life.

Your loving presence is God's loving presence in life. With loving presence comes joy. It makes life sparkle. In Acts 2:28 King David sings of the joy of God's presence: "You will make me full of gladness with your presence." Psalm 84:10 proclaims, "For a day in your court is better than a thousand elsewhere." A day in God's presence is better than going through life year after year on automatic pilot, unaware, and lacking presence, not experiencing that God is present in this place.

At a recent all-day meditation hosted by New River Zen Community, we spent the day in silence, alternately doing sitting and walking meditation periods, taking breaks for tea and lunch. It was a quiet Saturday and you could hear the birds outside singing, an occasional car going by, and now and then the bark of a dog or call of a child. During tea and lunch, the meditators strolled in the yard or sat on the porch enjoying the view of a nearby mountain. A few picked and ate cherries from an old cherry tree growing in the hedgerow. As usual we ended the day with a half-hour council circle. We sat carefully listening as members freely shared some insight or impression from the day or anything else they felt moved to say. I was surprised when one young man said in a very heartfelt way, "This was one of the best days of my life." This young man's comment speaks to the power of spending time simply being present with yourself and with others. A day of sitting together like this is a day of pure presence, rarely encountered even in a thousand years.

When you are fully present, not wandering off in thought or wishing that you were elsewhere, you are blessed with experiencing life, right here and now. You are enlivened by life's fleeting, fragile beauty. You feel fully at home in the world right where you are. "How lovely is your dwelling place, O Lord of hosts!" proclaims Psalm 84:1. In Zen, this is called returning to your "original dwelling place." Your original dwelling place is right here, wherever you are, and right now, when you are awake and present.

Every moment a clear bell
Calls us to complete presence
Uncluttered
Undistracted
Open, spacious
Joyful, loving
Fully here!

Opening to Love

Inclusive Love

INCLUSIVE LOVE means everyone is welcome and appreciated. People don't have to be just like you to be included in your circle. You extend your love to people regardless of tribe, race, nationality, gender, sexual orientation, or age. You respect differences, you are interested in diverse ways of living, and you enjoy being enriched by them.

The path of inclusive love comes to life in the story of Jesus and a woman from Samaria at Jacob's well. After traveling across the desert on foot, Jesus was thirsty. Having no bucket or rope to lower into the well, he asked a Samaritan woman if she would get him a drink of water. The woman was surprised by his request because Jewish people did not share things in common with Samaritans. In his interaction with the woman by the well, Jesus crossed cultural, religious, and gender barriers, setting an example for generations to come.

But Jesus's path of inclusive love is even more radical than this in his teaching in Matthew 5:44–45: "Love your enemies, and pray for those who persecute you." He models this behavior after God who "makes his sun rise on the evil and on the good, and sends rain on the righteous and the unrighteous." Inclusive love is a challenging spiritual practice.

In our time, the Dalai Lama is a living example of this kind of radical love. He refuses to be bitter and hateful toward the Chinese who brutally took over his country, sending him off to live in exile. He has not allowed his heart to be hardened, but instead he extends his love and prayers for the well-being of the people of China and for people everywhere. It is in the opening of the hearts of the Chinese and people everywhere that the Tibetan people will receive the justice and compassion that they deserve. For his wisdom and for his example, the Dalai Lama received the Nobel Peace Prize and has become a worldwide spiritual leader to people from many different religious backgrounds.

When I visited China, I had the opportunity to visit with many Chinese health care providers, professors, and students. When the topic of Tibet and the Dalai Lama came up in our casual conversations, they expressed surprise and puzzlement to hear about how popular the Dalai Lama is in the United States and other countries. They seemed to have limited access to information about this topic. They were unaware of his stature in the world and wondered why so many look up to him. There are still many barriers to open communication in the world, in cyberspace, and among people. Only by crossing over these barriers again and again, in love and goodwill, will they begin to dissolve.

There is a bridge in China where the great Zen Master Joshu lived during the eighth century. It is a beautiful, arched stone bridge. About this bridge, Joshu is famous for saying, "It lets asses cross. It lets horses cross." This is not unlike letting the sun shine and the rain fall on both the good and the bad. Joshu's bridge allows everyone to cross over. It does not discriminate. It is like inclusive love that allows everyone to cross over and be united.

While traveling in China with my Zen teacher, Roshi Robert Kennedy, we visited the monastery where Zen Master Dogen studied with his teacher Zen Master Rujing. While most of our group toured the main monastery, a few of us noticed a small sign pointing up the hill through the bamboo forest to the site of a smaller, older temple. When we got up to the monastery gate, it was locked and the complex seemed to be abandoned. But after we stood there for a while peering in through the gate, a monk appeared. Our friend Amy spoke to him in Chinese explaining that Rujing was a beloved ancestor in the lineage of Zen that we studied. United by our love for a common ancestor, he opened the gate and let us in to meditate together in that special place. Later we hiked back down the hill and the monk went out in the woods to harvest bamboo shoots.

Back home in Virginia, there is a small grove of bamboo behind the open barn on my daughter's property.

The bamboo roots grow right under the walls of the barn and up through the hard-packed dirt floor inside. It finds a way to grow over walls, under walls, and even through the smallest cracks. It's hard to wall life in or out.

Unfortunately, many religious organizations give lip service to inclusive love but continue to be unwilling to extend it to one group or another. As a woman I have experienced the sting of this reality. As a result, I currently attend a church that has a woman minister. It has been deeply healing for me to be part of an organization where women are not treated as second-class citizens but rather with full human dignity and full recognition of their leadership abilities. Pastor Karen Lane is smart, articulate, and—most of all—loving. Balancing her life as a wife and the mother of two small children with the demands of ministry is a living lesson for both mothers and fathers. Clearly, we are all poorer when 50 percent of the potential talent pool is excluded from any organization's leadership. We are all enriched by hearing both men's and women's realities and voices.

It is only in recent times that women have gained full recognition in many Buddhist organizations. When I became a Zen teacher, I received lineage papers that list a long succession of Zen ancestors extending over many generations from Buddha to the present day. My name was added onto the lineage after my teacher's name and was the only woman's name on the document. In the current generation there are many women Zen teachers, but in the past this has not been the case. The White Plum Asanga

and the American Zen Teachers' Association, two organizations of Zen teachers that I belong to, are both composed of about 50 percent men and 50 percent women.

My Zen teacher's own Zen teacher is Roshi Bernie
Glassman, who has been a leader in being inclusive.
Among the Zen teachers he has installed are men and
women, gay people and straight people, Catholic priests
and sisters, Jewish rabbis, Sufis, and Buddhists. This is in
keeping with Buddha's openness to people from traditions other than his own.

In the Zen tradition there is a story about a non-
Buddhist who comes to question Buddha. He asks Buddha to help him experience that which is beyond words
and non-words. In Buddha's presence, the non-Buddhist
gains deep insight into ultimate reality and is greatly
praised by Buddha. This surprises Buddha's cousin
and long time student, Ananda, who confronts Buddha about it. Buddha continues his praise of the non-
Buddhist. The direct experience of ultimate reality that
Buddha is teaching is beyond all division such as the
duality between words and non-words. Ultimate reality
is inclusive, encompassing everything. Everyone is welcome. Boundaries such as Buddhist and non-Buddhist
are crossed over.

Recently, I was riding home from a Zen workshop with
Zahra, a young woman from Iran who meditates regularly with New River Zen Community. She has a PhD in
engineering and works as an engineer here in the United
States. She said that she grew up in Iran and the Muslim

tradition of her family is still very meaningful to her. She also attends a local Christian church on Sundays and is planning to go on a mission trip to Africa with them next summer. In her heart she feels the truth and beauty in all of these traditions. There is no conflict. She does not agree when people view them as mutually exclusive. She is an example of an inclusive view that does not separate love into different camps. She represents a hope that, as the people, religions, and cultures of the world come together, our hearts will expand and our worldviews will become inclusive so we will appreciate and love one another.

Welcome everyone!
Rich and poor
Young and old
Women and men
Gay and straight
From every tribe and nation
From every noble tradition
Bring your gifts to the table.
Come celebrate our shared humanity.
Come honor our common ancestors—
Earth and stars
Human beings

Animal beings
Plant beings
Stone beings
All sentient and nonsentient
All hungry ghosts
Come join in love's feast.

Unbounded Love

SILENTLY SITTING in meditation is a way to cultivate a relaxed state of unbounded awareness. As you let go of thoughts, feelings, and sensations, your body and mind settle and your awareness opens and expands. You experience boundlessness—that your awareness is clear, bright, and vast like the sky. Boundaries or divisions dissolve. There is no separation: no separate things, no separate self. You directly experience the unbounded whole. The sky opens, your mind opens.

In Japanese the word for *mind* includes *heart*. Heart-mind: when the mind opens, the heart opens, and along with unbounded awareness comes unbounded love. Unbounded love can't be contained in concepts or expressed in words. Words and concepts divide and limit.

Saint Thomas Aquinas stopped writing his great work, the *Summa Theologiae*, after a mystical experience he had while celebrating liturgy on December 6, 1273. When urged to complete the work, he refused, saying, "I cannot go on . . . All that I have written seems to me like so much straw compared to what I have seen and what has been revealed to me." This story dramatically illustrates the limitations of words and concepts in comparison to what can be seen and revealed regarding realities such as God and love. No symbols, no concepts, no dogmas, no doctrines, no teachings, and no words are adequate in the realm of boundlessness. Saint Thomas remained silent, yet remaining silent doesn't do love justice either. In our everyday world we do use words to communicate, encourage, and inspire ourselves and others.

My great-great-great-aunt Anna Howard Shaw was the first woman ordained by the Methodist Protestant Church, a medical doctor, and an orator for the women's suffrage movement. Her words have been an inspiration to me; I am grateful that she took the time and had the courage to write them down so I can know her, long past her death in 1919. Aunt Anna wrote in her autobiography about being deeply moved by a note she received from her mentor, Susan B. Anthony, that ended with the closing, "With unbounded love and faith." This is where I first encountered the phrase "unbounded love," and it struck a chord in me.

Aunt Anna's preferred name for God was "the Infinite." In her view, Christianity, Zoroastrianism, Buddhism, Islam, Confucianism, and Hinduism all taught the same truth, which she called "infinite love." She said that reformers must be bathed in and led by "a great love for humanity, a love which nothing can quench. Which can endure all things and still trust with such an abiding faith that it saves, if not others, at least oneself." Love enables and empowers our humanity.

Infinite love, or unbounded love, is selfless love. It is God's love, not your own. My Zen teacher often says, "The moon has no light of its own." The light of the moon is a reflection of the sun's light, and yet moonlight inspires poets, saints, and lovers all around the world.

Radford University, where I work as a nursing professor, once hosted a delegation of administrators and professors from Nantong University in China. We were developing an exchange program between the two universities. A professor, who had been on one of our previous visits to Nantong University, entertained the group with a barbeque at his home out in the country. After dinner we all went on a hayride out through the grassy fields of grazing cattle to a nearby hilltop. As we watched the full moon rise, the head of the delegation began to sing a poem in Chinese. He translated it for us and said it was about two lovers far apart, one singing to the other, "The moon I see tonight is the same moon you see." We stood together looking out at the meadows and mountains in the moonlight, listening to his song about love that unites us even across great distances.

According to Luke 10:25–28, a lawyer once came to Jesus and asked what he needed to do to gain eternal life. Jesus responded, "What is written in the law? What do you read there?" The lawyer said, "You shall love the Lord your God with all your heart, and with all your soul, and with all your strength, and with all your mind; and your neighbor as yourself." Then Jesus said to him, "You have given the right answer; do this, and you will live."

This story speaks about unbounded love in two ways. First, you are challenged to give love your all: your whole heart, whole soul, whole strength, and whole mind. How big is your whole heart? Your open heart is unbounded and infinite. Heart, soul, strength, and mind are not separate entities; they are aspects of one whole selfless self that is not separate from the whole of life manifesting moment by moment.

Second, to love like this *is* eternal life. It isn't a matter of loving now and getting eternal life after you die. If you love wholeheartedly, you experience eternal life right here and now. Unbounded love is not bound by time. It is infinite and eternal.

Unbounded love has no beginning and no end to it. It transcends space and time, and although it is vast, it is contained in each small act of love.

Last summer, a few days before my mother died, I took my seven-year-old granddaughter, Elise, to visit her in the nursing home. On our way there we stopped at a bakery. Elise picked out a chocolate chip cookie for herself and then asked, "What kind of cookie does Nanny like?" I told her Nanny likes cookies with fruit in them, so Elise picked out an oatmeal raisin cookie and took it to Nanny. She sat in a chair beside the bed and they ate their cookies together.

After Nanny died family members were sitting around talking about the last time each of us had seen her. Elise said, "I saw her on Saturday. I took her a cookie!" It was a small act of unbounded love because each precious drop of love contains the whole ocean of love. Unbounded love is not abstract; it is always particular.

Working as a neonatal intensive care nurse, I saw this happening right before my eyes, when standing ready in the delivery room during high-risk deliveries. I saw that many parents had fallen in love with their infant even before the baby was born and were giving their all—all of their heart, soul, strength, and mind—to bring their tiny baby safely and lovingly into the world. Giving birth to a baby is one of the most spiritual experiences many people have in life. As the parents first behold the face of their new baby, the love in the room is palpable and transforming. Everyone is full of life and the parents experience a love for their child they know is for always and forever. Love is life-giving.

Love also gives birth to an ocean of tears. There is a story about a Zen master who went to a house in the nearby village to be with a family whose father had just died. As the Zen master sat there crying with the family, a man in town noticed him weeping and said, "I would have thought you had gone beyond this." The Zen master replied, "This is how I go beyond it." The Zen master expressed his love for the man and for the family by sharing their grief and common humanity. There was no boundary between their love and grief and his. The story is like the story of Jesus weeping when he hears his friend Lazarus has died. When we love deeply, we feel deeply; our own pain and the pain of others are not separate.

Opening to the whole of life, just as it is, your heart-mind realizes unbounded awareness and unbounded love. Standing in the moonlight, love quenches the thirst of all living beings.

Boundless expanded vision includes the whole universe.

I am the burning bush, on fire with love, but not consumed.

Feeling deeply my own joy and pain

Letting tears flow

Letting waves of feeling swell

Rising and falling

Breathing clear, refined air

Alive from head to toe

Younger than I've ever been before

I am reborn with a heart that is wide open.

Unconditional Love

WE YEARN for unconditional love, to be loved with no strings attached, to be loved no matter what choices we make in life, to be loved for who we are regardless of what we say or do.

The love of parents for their children is as close as most people come to the ideal of unconditional love. Evolution has biologically ingrained this love of parents for their offspring to ensure the survival of the species. This genetic tendency is supported by all that we learn from our culture about the importance of family. Yet even in the case of parent-child love there are many factors that sabotage it, such as substance abuse, mental illness, and self-centeredness. It is a tragic reality that many children experience neglect and abuse rather than love from their parents. Even in loving homes, often the ideal of unconditional love is not reached.

So we turn to romantic relationships, hoping to find unconditional love. Even when it feels at first that we have finally found the love we are longing for, it doesn't stand the test of time. High divorce rates offer ample evidence that the expectation of unconditional love, love that lasts a lifetime, turns out to be unrealistic for far too many men and women.

The problem with this approach to unconditional love is that you are thinking of love as a thing or commodity and you are hoping to get enough of it. More often than not this viewpoint leads to great disappointment and suffering.

Love is not a thing. You are not a thing. You are not a container that needs to be filled up with love, like a cup or a bowl or a bucket. When you see completely through the illusion of self as a fixed entity or thing, you directly experience that you are not separate from ultimate reality or God. God is love. You are not separate from God's love. You are God's love. If you do not realize this, you will endlessly long to receive unconditional love from others and you will be unable to give unconditional love to others.

Selfless love is abundant love. It is spacious and generous. It is not like selfish love that expects something in return. Selfish love tries to control, and ends up destroying love, because love can't be controlled. Love is free. It can't be bought or sold. Selfless love is freeing. It is based in being free from a small, limited, separate sense of self. When you are free, you empower others to be free. You allow others the freedom to choose what they think and feel. This requires the generosity of letting go of what you want and opening to the perspective of others. Your vision expands and becomes more spacious in order to include your views and the views of others.

Insight into selflessness is just the first step in opening

to God's love and living a life of selfless love. Developing your ability to pay attention during meditation and during daily life cultivates this insight. This same attention is then needed, on an ongoing basis, to embody selfless love to ever-greater degrees in your life. This is why daily meditation is a lifelong practice. As human beings we have been evolving for thousands of years. We are physiologically and culturally programmed for survival. Some of this conditioning leads us toward forming loving bonds with others such as infants, children, and family members to ensure our mutual survival. However, much of our conditioning is aggressive and competitive to ensure our own survival over the survival of others. It is this aggressive and competitive conditioning that we need to become increasingly aware of so it does not overshadow our expression of love.

I became clearly aware of some of my survival instinct one day while on a trip to Alaska. I hiked off into the woods a short distance to take a picture. As I was standing there admiring the magnificent mountains rising into the clear blue sky, two bear cubs came sauntering through the brush toward me. They were so cute, but I immediately thought, "Oh no! Their mother will be right behind them." I raced to the car as fast as I could go, not wanting to come face-to-face with mother bear.

Sometimes when I perceive that someone is attacking one of my family members or someone in my care who is vulnerable in some way, I come face-to-face with the mother bear within me. I feel adrenaline rush into my system as I go into mother-bear mode. Anger arises in my body, and I am ready to attack. Aware of this conditioned response, I take a few breaths, calm down for a minute, and assess the situation before overreacting to protect those in my care.

Although unconditional love is the ideal, there is deep-seated conditioning within us that we need to grow more aware of in order to move toward making love a reality. Much of this conditioning remains beyond our awareness; it is essential to acknowledge this fact as well. This is part of the mystery—the not knowing—discussed earlier in this book. The humility that goes with not knowing helps us to be as aware as possible, doing our best to live a kinder, more loving life.

There are many opportunities large and small that pop up every day to teach us how to be more loving. One Saturday morning I got up early to go watch my seven-year-old granddaughter play basketball in the local school gym. The kids did their best to figure out the rules of the game and dribble the length of the court without losing the ball somewhere along the way. At one point in the game, my granddaughter tried to get the ball from a player on the other team. The other little girl tried to dodge, fell down, hurt her knee, and started to cry. My granddaughter started to cry along with her. The coaches gathered around to make sure the girl who fell was okay and soon she stood up ready to continue playing. I heard them ask my granddaughter why she was crying. They told her she hadn't done anything wrong; they assured her that what she did was within the rules of the game. She was doing exactly what she was supposed to do and shouldn't feel bad about it. I was interested to see her natural response of sympathetic pain. She cried because another little girl got hurt. Everyone told her that it was just part of the game. She needed to toughen up, stop crying, and play the game. I was watching cultural conditioning take place before my very eyes. I wanted to run out onto the court and praise my granddaughter for her compassion for the little girl on the other team.

In his classic book *The Art of Loving*, Erich Fromm points out the need for both unconditional and conditional love. Conditional love involves parents teaching their children the rules, discipline, expectations, and consequences they will encounter in life so they grow up to be competent and independent adults in the world. Conditional love is worked for and earned. Although it sounds paradoxical, unconditional love and conditional love are complementary, and when in balance, they work together to promote optimal human development.

Over the course of my career I've taught nursery school, first grade, and college. One of the greatest joys in teaching young children is that you can set up an environment for them at school that cultivates respect and caring for each other's feeling. Young children can learn from the start not to hit, say mean things, or take toys away from other children. When the environment is organized, consistent, and caring, they learn to ask nicely for what they want and to tell others when their feelings are hurt so situations can be resolved. Their loving innocence is supported.

An environment of caring can also be cultivated at the college level, but by then more previous conditioning has occurred so the challenge is greater. Most of the students are civil and caring, but not all. It is sad to see the incivility and bullying that goes on even among some of our society's most educated people. The same is true in the workplace where many people endure hostile work environments day after day. Hostility can easily become a habit. A commitment needs to be made to bring unconditional love, respect, and caring for the well-being of others back to the fore so it can bring balance to the realities of demanding, competitive school and work situations. Conditioned love needs to be reconditioned and reconstructed to harmonize with unconditional love.

Love shines
Moment by moment
Conditioning eclipses the sun
Still love blazes
Now, always
Warmth and light endure

Wise Love

OFTEN IN THE Buddhist tradition, wisdom and compassion are said to be like the two wings of a great bird. Both wings are needed for the bird to fly; either one alone is not enough. The two wings work together in harmony to produce the freedom of flight.

Wisdom and compassion go together like wisdom and love; both are needed to function as a loving person in the world. Wisdom is the realization that you are not a discrete, isolated self. You are larger than your limited, separate self, which is not the self that engages in wise love. When you experience that you are one with the larger reality, you are able to love wisely. Wise love is selfless love. It is seeing that everything is interconnected, the functioning of one whole ultimate reality or God. Wise love arises from experiencing the loving nature of ultimate reality as it manifests in the world. You experience that God is love and that you are not separate from God's love. Wise love is sharing God's love, which is abundant and unlimited. It is not the limited love of your small ego-self.

Wise love is not foolish or blind. It does not deny the reality of life; it doesn't deny the small, limited self with its sense of incompleteness and lack that results in feelings of loneliness, isolation, and vulnerability. Much of the greed, meanness, and ignorant behavior in the world are attempts to assuage these feelings. The self-centered ego has a desire to survive at all costs. These strong survival instincts are genetically encoded in humans from thousands of years of evolution. The costs of continued enactment of fight or flight survival instincts, in current contexts where they no longer serve a productive purpose, range from individual angst and misery to holocaust and war. Wise love is love that is accompanied by an awareness of the complexity of these realities in yourself, others, and the world at large. Wise love acknowledges the good and the evil, the easy and the difficult, the happy and the sad, wisdom and ignorance, love and hatred, all as interconnected manifestations of the whole. Wise love embraces these dichotomies yet sees beyond them to what cannot be divided. Wise love unifies, heals, and makes whole.

Wise love sees and feels that you are not separate from others. You and all others are manifestations of the same larger whole. In knowing both your small ego-self with all its feelings of vulnerability as well as your unity with a larger reality, you have compassion for your own limitations and compassion for the limitations of others. Your identity as a manifestation of ultimate reality allows you to experience that you are not separate from everyone and everything. You are joined in God's love.

Wise love is more than a feeling. Sometimes in life you may be swept away by a strong feeling of love and later wake up to find yourself asking, "What was I thinking?" The answer is, of course, "I wasn't thinking." Or perhaps you weren't thinking clearly. In retrospect you can see many warning signs that trouble was likely to lay ahead, but at the time you foolishly chose to ignore them. This may have been a youthful mistake from which you can learn, but sometimes the damage resulting from a relationship like this can be great; sometimes the pattern of falling madly in love and having it turn out badly is repeated over and over in your life. These painful experiences and patterns underscore the message that love and wisdom need to go hand in hand. In loving wisely, you don't throw reason to the wind. Love is not just a wild carefree feeling. True love includes caring deeply for the well-being of the one you love.

Often it's hard to figure out how to respond in a loving way to some of the complex and difficult situations that come up in life. Your feelings are just one piece of the puzzle. Both your positive and negative feelings need to be acknowledged and honored. In addition, listen carefully to your gut feelings and your intuition. The feelings of the heart need to be balanced with the reasoning of your mind. This includes both using your common sense and gaining further knowledge about the matter under consideration.

If a decision is particularly perplexing, seek the support and help of others to shed new light on the matter. This may include family members, friends, professional counselors or therapists, members of your spiritual community, or respected elders who have valuable life experience to share. Sometimes in the Native American tradition when there is an important decision to be made, the tribal members sit in a circle listening to one another as each is moved to speak. This may last several hours or several days before a course of action presents itself and is agreed upon. In the Native American tradition ultimate reality or God is sometimes called the "great mystery." It is beyond our human capacity to know the correct answer or solution to all the complex problems that we face in life, but we are required to do our best, united with each other and the great mystery. It is essential to have the patience to sit silently together listening to what is revealed.

One of the best known Hindu scriptures, the *Bhagavad Gita,* provides guidance and comfort in facing situations in life that challenge our ability to act in a loving way amid complex life circumstances. In this long poem, the warrior Arjuna, while on the battlefield preparing for battle, engages in conversation with Lord Krishna regarding the conflict he has between his duty as a warrior and the fact that soon he will be killing family members and friends who are among the enemy ranks. He is advised by Lord Krishna that he must honor his duty as a warrior and fight, but he must not do this with malice or pleasure. Arjuna is instructed to do all that he does with an attitude of love. The lesson in this is that we may face dilemmas in life where it is not possible to do what is best for everyone involved. When this is the case, don't act with hatred and malice. Our basic attitude toward others and toward all living beings and the earth needs to be an attitude of love. To the extent possible, we do our best to do no harm and to do good for others. When this is not possible, we do all that we do with love and compassion. In this way we honor our ultimate reality as the love of God manifesting in all that exists in this complex world in which we live.

The complexities of wise love are described well in 1 Corinthians 13:1–6, a passage from the Bible that is often read at weddings. "If I speak in the tongues of mortals and of angels, but do not have love, I am a noisy gong or clanging cymbal. And if I have prophetic powers, and understand all mysteries and all knowledge, and if I have all faith, so as to remove mountains, but do not have love, I am nothing." It begins by emphasizing that love is greater than words, special powers, or any knowledge that we may possess. Love is who we are; without love we are nothing. It is not the love that we receive that is being spoken of here but rather the love that we give, the love that we live, the love that we are.

The passage goes on to give us a list of attributes of wise love. "Love is patient; love is kind; love is not envious or boastful or arrogant or rude. It does not insist on its own way; it is not irritable or resentful; it does not rejoice in wrongdoing, but rejoices in the truth." Love is patient with yourself and others. It forgives mistakes and allows time to try again. Love is not in a hurry; moment by moment it is eternal. Love is kind; it becomes real in your caring acts and the compassion you express when another is suffering. Love is content, humble, and polite.

In a loving atmosphere, civility flourishes. Love respects multiple perspectives and does not insist on "my way or the highway." Love extinguishes the fires of anger and resentment. Love rejoices in doing what is in the other's best interest and in being a positive influence that ripples out to the ends of the universe.

Wisdom and love walk hand in hand
No separation
Whole heart, whole mind, every cell
Not crazy wisdom
Not blind love
Clear eyed
Joyful caring
Sweet embrace

Embodied Love

SOME OF THE greatest gifts of Eastern religious traditions to those raised in the Western world are forms of
meditation and prayer that involve not just the mind and
heart but the whole body. For many in the West, meditation was traditionally considered reflection on scripture
or an inspiring passage from a book. You sat in your easy
chair or at your desk and read from a book of daily devo-
tions or some other spiritual writing. Then you sat quietly
for a while thinking about its meaning. Eastern forms of
meditation are not just thinking about spiritual matters;
they involve the body as well. The posture you assume
and the act of paying attention to your breathing make
the body an integral part of meditation. In Zen meditation
you are urged to be alert and attentive with every cell in
your body. You become aware of the body, not as a thing,
but as a continuously changing flow of energy. This contributes to the direct experience of selflessness discussed
in the first section of this book.

Meditation practice is not limited to the time you spend
in sitting meditation. Walking meditation not only gives
you a chance to stretch your legs in the midst of a long

meditation session, it helps you learn how to maintain the same alert attentiveness of sitting meditation while in motion. During walking meditation, rather than focus your attention on your breathing, you instead maintain an awareness of walking—just the sensation of moving, or the feeling of your foot coming in contact with the ground. Your eyes are cast down at the ground in front of you and you are not distracted by looking all around. You simply walk without drifting off in thought or daydreaming. You walk with awareness. You occupy your body and become aware of the beauty and magnificence of just walking.

As a nurse, I work with many people who are unable to walk for one reason or another, as a result of an injury, due to weakness after surgery, or from the frailty of old age. I am always moved by the skill of the therapists and the determination of the young children especially, who learn to walk despite tremendous challenges. Walking is a miracle. During walking meditation you take time to experience and appreciate the miracle of walking.

Learning to be aware during sitting and walking meditation helps you develop the ability to be aware during daily life. When you drive the car, be present and aware, with your hands on the steering wheel and your eyes on the road in front of you. Living in your body, aware of what you are doing with your hands and eyes, brings you into the present moment. Too much of the time, we drive in a trance, daydreaming, on automatic pilot. Or even worse, many people drive while distracted, talking on the phone or texting. There are many opportunities in life to practice being more aware and present, to practice living in your body.

When you take a shower, be aware of the warm water spraying from the showerhead onto your face and flowing down over your body. Be aware of the fragrance of the shampoo and shower gel. Feel the gentle pressure of your fingers massaging your scalp. Enjoy the feeling of the towel rubbing your skin as you dry off. Take a moment to feel fully cleansed and refreshed. Treat your body with respect and appreciation, giving it the attention it needs.

It is good to take care of your body and appreciate all that you experience through your body. However, it is also important not to over-identify with your body as being who you are, or view it as a thing that belongs to you. Our culture emphasizes having a beautiful body by using lots of cosmetics and products, exercising, and eating just the right foods and supplements. This needs to be brought back into balance with awareness that the body is not a thing, it is not a possession, it is not your identity; it's rather a moment-by-moment manifestation of the formless ultimate reality taking form in the relative world. The formless takes form in the body. Love takes form in the body. The formless and form are not separate realities. From a nondual perspective, it is not "me" and "my body"; there is just this one miraculous, magnificent life.

Love is embodied. You feel love throughout your body. It is enlivening. You can feel it in your eyes, lips, mouth, heart, breasts, belly, hips, genitals, thighs, knees, feet, arms, and hands. Different kinds of love are felt differently in various areas of your body and they ripple throughout your whole body. You also feel hurt and tension throughout your body. When you inhabit your body and are aware of how your body feels, you are better able to empathize with the feelings of others and respond to them with care, kindness, and love.

A neighbor, Larry, died recently of cancer. Larry had been a soldier in Vietnam. Because the Vietnam veterans did not receive the welcome and gratitude they deserved when they returned home from war, each year on Veteran's Day, for the past twenty-five years, my husband Charles stopped by or called Larry on the phone to say, "Welcome home, soldier." Over the years they were close friends to one another, so as Larry's illness progressed and he spent most of his time resting on the sofa, Charles would go sit and talk with him whenever the light on the end table in the living room was turned on, indicating that Larry felt well enough for company. The last day Charles visited Larry, as they sat together on the sofa, Larry reached out and took his hand. When Charles got ready to leave, he stood up, but Larry would not let go, so Charles sat back down again and the two men just sat together for a while holding hands. Love is expressed through the body—two men who had never held hands before sat silently hand in hand.

In the Christian world, Christmas is an occasion filled with great joy because it celebrates God's incarnation in the human form of Jesus. Incarnation is not just true for Jesus; it is a reality for each of us. The formless God manifests in human form. Humanity and divinity are united in the body. In this sense there is just one body. We are all members of one body.

There is a beautiful verse written by Zen Master Soju included at the end of *The Gateless Gate*. It says:

How does my hand compare with the Buddha's hand?
Groping for the pillow at my back, I could feel it.
In spite of myself I burst out laughing.
From the first, the whole body is the hand.

A Christian might say, "Your hands are Christ's hands in the world." A Buddhist might say, "Your hands are Buddha's hands in the world." This verse asks, "How does your hand compare with Buddha's hand?" to point toward the realization that your hand *is* Buddha's hand. Buddha and you are manifestations of the same ultimate reality.

Ultimate reality manifests everywhere, in all the parts of the body. This verse speaks of reaching out for a pillow, feeling it, and bursting out laughing. When you laugh you feel it throughout your body. Your face changes shape, your body shakes, and the sound of laughter vibrates out through your vocal chords. Once a friend of mine told a joke he thought was so funny that he fell back onto the sofa holding his stomach and kicking his feet in the air as he laughed at his own joke. His whole body laughed.

The final line of this verse says, "the whole body is the hand." This is saying that not only do all the parts of the body work together in harmony as one whole, but also that each part contains the whole. In his commentary on this verse Zen Master Yamada Roshi distinguishes between the whole body, which is your body, and the entire body, which includes the whole universe. You are not separate from the grass, trees, mountains, rivers, sky, stars, and moon. Your body is the entire universe. God's love is embodied in the whole universe. You are the incarnation of God's love. God's love unifies all of creation.

Love comes to life in your fingertips
Each cell of your body is love
All the interstitial spaces are love
Love extends out into intergalactic space
Throughout space and time
It shines forth in ten thousand stars and faces
To awaken us

Loving Life

L OVING LIFE is your overall sense of joy in life. You are glad to be alive. You appreciate the opportunity to be alive on this earth for a while. You embrace both happy times and difficulties as parts of the fabric of life that give your life color and texture. You face losses and challenges with courage and view life as an adventure. You don't get bogged down in anxiety, rumination, and depression. Your courage, vitality, and love of life are felt by those around you.

It is sad that so many people these days are depressed. According to the World Health Organization, depression is the third leading cause of disability globally. Substance abuse is also in the top twenty. Often substance abuse is a person's attempt to dull or escape the pain of living; it can be viewed as self-destructive behavior or gradual suicide. There are many factors that contribute to these illnesses including biological, psychological, cultural, and spiritual factors. Treatment requires multiple interventions to address the various contributing factors. One useful treatment strategy is to help people regain their sense of enjoyment of the simple pleasures of life.

One day I was at the hospital supervising a group of brand new nursing students. They were excited to finally get to the hospital and take care of real patients after two long years in college completing the prerequisite chemistry, microbiology, and pathophysiology. One student was assigned to care for an elderly woman who was severely depressed. I assisted the student in getting the woman safely into the tub and giving her a bath. At first the woman didn't want to take a bath, but she really needed her hair washed and her skin carefully cleaned. With patience we were finally able to coax her into taking a bath. She began to relax a bit as she sat in the sudsy water while the student gently washed her hair. But it wasn't until we sang a song for her, as the student washed her back, that she smiled ever so slightly. After her bath, we went for a walk outside in the garden surrounding the unit. The student and I stood on each side of her since she was unsteady on her feet at times. As we strolled along the garden path, I could see new life coming back into her face. I asked her, "Which of the flowers growing here in the garden is your favorite?" With energy in her voice she replied, "I love every one of them!" Hearing this I knew that the bath, the song, the walk, the flowers, and the student's caring attention had helped her take a step toward healing.

It is important to receive life, moment by moment, as the precious gift that it is. Embracing life in this way, you experience your own value. Appreciating your own value is not selfish or conceited. Valuing yourself is not limited to your small ego-self. Truly valuing yourself is expanded by the insight that you are not separate from everyone and everything else. In valuing yourself you value the whole of life and each and every person. You directly experience that life is precious, each person is precious, and you are precious. This attitude toward life enables you to treat yourself, others, all living things, the earth, and the sky with love and respect.

A life of love is a life of abundance. This is a key Christian teaching. In John 10:10, Jesus said, "I come that they may have life and have it abundantly." It is unfortunate when this is interpreted materialistically. Abundance of life does not mean unlimited consumption. It does not give license to produce and buy more and more useless trinkets. Having more and more things breeds unhappiness rather than satisfaction in life. It is in simplicity and love that abundance of life is found, that you are freed from selfish greed to live fully with love.

Meditation can be viewed as a process of simplification that leads to a rich and abundant life. In meditation you simply sit in silence, content to be in the present moment just as it is, aware of your breathing. The environment around you is cleared of unneeded clutter and the endless thoughts in your mind are allowed to abate. You set aside time to experience the simple peace and joy of being alive, one breath at a time.

After a daylong meditation retreat, or even more so, after a weekend or weeklong retreat, you will find that you've become very sensitive to the exquisite beauty of life all around you. You are startled by a leaf, with its rich green color and intricate system of veins. Previously you often missed seeing whole trees, not to mention individual leaves. You are amazed by the sweet taste of a single grape, as it pops in your mouth, releasing its juiciness; previously you often gulped down a whole meal without tasting a single bite. You feel tender toward the feelings expressed on the faces of the people you encounter, appreciating their humanity and not just passing them by unnoticed. You are awake, marveling at life swirling around and within you. You are not separate from life itself and life becomes full and vibrant.

We can regain a childlike delight in life. Often on rainy days my grandchildren beg to go out and play in the puddles left behind in the wake of a thunderstorm. This is an easy request to fulfill—as long as I make sure they're not wearing anything I don't want to get wet or muddy. They start out wading into the puddle to float a few toy boats around. Shortly this progresses to splashing each other and me. I act surprised when water comes my way, getting my clothes wet, and then join in splashing them back. We laugh and squeal, getting wetter and wetter. Before long one of them sits right down in the puddle and bursts out laughing. Playing in mud puddles is a great life lesson in making the most of what life brings your way and in sharing the joy of life with others. It is important for children and adults to feel the goodness, playfulness, silliness, and sweetness of life and be glad that they were born.

The other day I was watching a television show that included performances and interviews with members of some of the old rock-and-roll bands from the fifties and sixties. A friend called me on the phone to tell me to watch the show because it was so much fun. One of the performers being interviewed said that it was really meaningful to him to continue touring because the music brought back so many feelings for the people in the audience. He wanted to let his generation know that even now, in their older years, they can still feel as alive as they did in their youth.

It is easy to take for granted or ignore the good parts of life and get into the habit of complaining and blaming. Habitual complaining generates more irritation and discontent. Blaming fuels resentment. Although our complaints may be legitimate, constant complaining doesn't solve the problem and ends up weighing ourselves down and dragging others down with us. Instead of blaming others for how we feel, it is better to assume responsibility for how we feel and choose to do what we need to do to enjoy life while we have it.

There is a Zen chant that says, "Life and death are of supreme importance. Time swiftly passes by and opportunity is lost. Each of us must strive to awaken. Awaken! Take heed. Do not squander your life." Life is of supreme value, your life and the life of others. Life is short and nobody knows when death will come. This chant urges you to wake up right now and appreciate your life. Don't waste your time complaining, blaming, and arguing. Don't spend your time generating more misery for yourself and others. Don't waste this opportunity to walk, run, dance, sing, cry, and laugh here on this earth this very day. Don't spend your time in a daze missing the beauty and poignant drama of nature and humanity within and around you. Wake up and live your life fully. Wake up and love life.

When I die, I hope my family and friends don't just say that I was loving, hard-working, smart, and did many things to help others. I hope they also say that I loved life, that I taught others to love life, and that we had a lot of fun together.

Love wakes up in the morning.
In love with the rain,
in love with the coo-coo-coo of the mourning doves,
in love with the warmth of my bed,
in love with life.

The body breathes love.
Love in the eyes and hands.
Love in the fingertips and toes.
Energized, alive.

Compassionate Action

What Selfless Love Isn't

SELFLESS LOVE is not a life of self-sacrificing martyrdom. Self-sacrifice is giving up what you need or
want for the good of others. Selflessness is not the same as
self-sacrifice because it is based on the direct experience
that there is no separate self to begin with. There is no
separate self that needs to suffer or be denied for the sake
of others. Self and others are not separate. They rise and
fall together. The separate self is seen for what it is—an
illusion. Letting go of the separate self is letting go of the
limitations that come with the view of the self as a fixed
entity or thing. Selflessness is not suffering; it is liberation from suffering. You regain your fluidity and ability to
change and transform your life. You acknowledge that the
ego-self has its purpose—to help you think, plan, orga-
nize, and function in the world—but are aware that it is
not who you are in your wholeness. Selflessness restores
your sense of wholeness and your ability to balance your
own needs and the needs of others.

Many people fear that if they love selflessly, they will
be at risk for burnout or compassion fatigue, but true selfless love does not tire you out. Actually, the exhausted,

dried-up feeling of burnout is a clear message that you are not experiencing selflessness and you are not loving from the experience that you *are* rather than *have* God's love. The love of the small, limited self is itself small and limited. When you endlessly try to give your love to others, as if love is a commodity you own and decide to dispense, you do run out. You run out of energy, run out of enjoyment in life, and even lose the original feeling of love that motivated you in the beginning.

Sometimes we cause ourselves anxiety, thinking about all that needs to be done to love our family, friends, coworkers, those in need in the community, and people all over the world who are in dire circumstances. It is overwhelming and exhausting just to think about it. Thinking that you can and must accomplish all of this is a grandiose delusion of the small ego-self. Thinking like this is stressful and exhausting. You must recognize these thoughts and feelings for what they are; they are egotistical.

Selfless love realizes that there is no separate self that needs to love endlessly in order to demonstrate its worth. As a manifestation of the whole, as a manifestation of God's love, and as a human being on this earth, you are already of immeasurable value. You do not need to earn God's love. It was your first birthday gift; you've had it from the start. You are God's love now and forever. You just need to open to it and realize it. When the separate self tries to earn love by constantly working to fix all the world's problems at home and abroad, it becomes unbalanced and ends in exhaustion, depleted of its limited resources. When the whole self loves, it is constantly changing, revitalizing, reconnecting, and realizing that it is unbounded love and possibility. Loving with a sense of your true identity brings balance and harmony to your life and the lives of others.

Maintaining awareness of your true identity requires time in your daily schedule for spiritual practice such as meditation. Meditation is like hitting the refresh button on your computer. The small ego-self is sneaky and comes creeping in over and over again, trying to take over your life. You need time and awareness to clear the screen and start fresh. Selfless love is not ignoring your own needs in order to meet the needs of others. Selfless love reveals your needs and allows you to respond to them with care and concern. In addition to time for daily spiritual practice, you need exercise, sleep, nutritious food, water, affection, and play. Selfless love acknowledges these human needs in yourself and others.

Selfless love is not about always doing for others. Doing for others needs to be balanced with caring for yourself and developing your talents. Selfless love does not mean obsequiously receding into the background. At times, selfless love may require you to fearlessly step forward and take the lead. When you let go of the small, limited self, you let go of the need to always gain the approval of others and your compulsion to always do for others. Letting go of limiting views of yourself not only liberates you, it empowers others, and brings balance back into relationships. When you stop doing everything for others, they learn how to do for themselves, and they gain the dignity and satisfaction that comes from being a contributing member of a family, work group, organization, or community.

Selfless love does not mean being a doormat and letting people walk all over you. It doesn't mean that you don't stand up for yourself. Selfless love embraces the value and dignity of every person—including yourself. You express yourself assertively to get your needs met while respecting the needs and feelings of others. You are honest without dwelling in negativity, complaining, or unconstructive criticism. You are kind, but truthful.

Selfless love is not indulgence. It sets limits on your own behavior and the behavior of others. It requires self-discipline from you and cultivates it in others. Selfless love does not ignore cause and effect; it is aware of the consequences of your chosen behaviors for yourself and others. As I am writing this, I just ate a piece of chocolate to keep myself going. To indulge in a little chocolate is okay and adds joy to life. But a lack of self-discipline— eating a whole box of chocolates—will certainly lead to consequences that are not loving toward myself. Selfless love sets appropriate limits.

Although selfless love includes the direct experience of nonseparation and no boundaries, it also establishes appropriate boundaries in life. For example, we each need some time to relax and be alone. This can be accomplished by announcing that you will be away for the weekend and won't be accessing your computer or talking on the phone until Monday morning. Leaving the number of someone to contact in case of emergency also helps. Or you can say, "I am going into my room to rest for an hour. I will see you at six for supper." These kinds of boundaries enhance your ability to be more responsive to others when you return to interact with them again. It is a loving thing to do, since it prevents you from becoming exhausted and emotionally unavailable.

My husband grew up on a farm where they plowed with horses. When he was eight years old they got their first tractor and sold the horses. His father often said that although the tractor was meant to make life easier, in some ways it made farming more demanding. Plowing with horses meant his dad had to stop periodically to rest the horses. While the horses rested, he rested. However, the tractor never needed a rest so everyone on the farm just kept working. People are more like horses than tractors. We need to take regular breaks. This has become even clearer in the age of computers and cellphones, which allow family members, friends, and bosses to expect you to be available at all times. The reality remains that we are animals, not machines. We need breaks from all of the technology and demands of life. Selfless love does not mean that you never get a break.

Selfless love does not mean that you have an unrealistically rosy-eyed attitude toward life. Selfless love is clear eyed. It acknowledges what is, just as it is—including good, evil, happiness, sadness, wonder, horror, ambition, laziness, humility, arrogance, honesty, and deceit in yourself, others, and the world. Life includes problems, mistakes, and difficult decisions. Selfless love affirms our ability to solve problems creatively, learn from mistakes, and carefully make difficult decisions. The Upayakausalya Sutra has a story in which Buddha, in one of his past lives as a ship captain, must respond to a robber who is about to kill the five hundred merchants onboard his ship in order to steal their goods. To save the merchants and prevent the robber from experiencing the repercussions of committing such a terrible massacre, the Buddha, as ship captain, killed the robber with a spear. Although killing is against Buddhist principles, not doing so would have allowed the robber to murder five hundred people. The captain's action is an example of selfless love because it was not done for any selfish motive; the captain thoroughly considered all of his options, and he chose the most compassionate course of action under the circumstances. Killing was not right, but it was the best choice in this difficult situation.

Selfless love is not angry or self-righteous. The ship captain did not act in anger or to punish the robber; he acted out of love to protect the merchants. Sadly, I have known several very angry peace activists over the course of my life, whose anger caused tremendous personal suffering for themselves and for the people closest to them.

If you are not in touch with the love that is who you really are, you are not able to radiate the love, peace, and joy you hope to create in the world. Selfless love is not being righteous or right; it is respecting and honoring all aspects of reality, our own and others', and reaching out in love.

Selfless love.
No martyrdom
No exhaustion
No self-righteousness
No merit.

Selfless love.
Neither saccharine
Nor passive.
Neti, neti
Not this, not this.
Muuuuuuuuuu
Noooooooooo.

Then what?
Self-emptying.
Pouring out.

Being Love

THINKING ABOUT the meaning of the word *love* or imagining that you are generating love won't bring it to you. God's vast love is beyond anything a human being can imagine. You experience it by opening your mind and heart, and every cell in your body, to what is, and to who you are, right here and now. Sitting silently in meditation is one way to open to the subtle reality of love, which pervades the whole universe. Love is boundless and full of infinite possibilities.

Being love is realizing that you *are* love and then acting in accord with what you are. You are God's vast, infinite love. When you experience this, you are liberated to act in loving ways both small and large. Being love is the wellspring of compassionate action. Compassionate action is not just helping others and doing good deeds, it is uniting with others in love. Compassionate action is simultaneously giving and receiving—mutually sharing—humanity and love.

Being love naturally expresses itself in loving action and seeks to create harmony. Contentment is not found by basking in your own individual experience of love and bliss. Love reaches out to join with others for mutual enlightenment and well-being. Love radiates out to the corners of the world to bring joy and peace to all.

Being love manifests in compassionate action that is balanced and not compulsive. There is no need to feel pressured to do more and more. You are responsible for doing all that you can, but you are not responsible for doing everything. Love is not an isolated venture. It can only be done in union with all. Being love realizes the power and liberation of this union.

Even amid difficulty, crisis, and chaos, you can choose to be a beacon of light, life, humanity, and love. Do what you are able to do to help out under the circumstances, but when there is nothing you can do to alleviate a problem, improve the situation by facing it with empathy and love for all those involved. As a nurse, I often care for patients with chronic or terminal illnesses. The reality is that we still lack the medical knowledge needed to cure many illnesses. In these situations, the best we can do is treat the symptoms in order to keep the patient as comfortable as possible, while maximizing the quality of his or her life. You can also be with the patient in an empathetic, loving way to accompany him or her through the experience of life, illness, and death, providing human companionship. Compassionate action includes both performing loving actions and just being there with and for another.

Being love leads to compassionate action that is not drudgery, obligation, or duty. It is a privilege and a delight. Compassionate action is a joyful, creative expression of who you are. Compassionate action takes discipline and hard work, but when undertaken with awareness that you *are* love, there is spontaneity, creativity, excitement, surprise, and amazement as well. You join in co-creating beauty, healing, and love on earth.

Being love awakens the sense of the sacred in your own life and in the lives of others. This sense of the sacred is enlivening. Compassionate action is infused with this liveliness. There is a well-known hymn that says, "Joyful, joyful, we adore Thee, God of Glory, Lord of love; Hearts unfold like flowers before Thee, opening to the sun above." When you engage in compassionate action, you adore God who manifests in yourself and others. With each step you take you are aware that you are on holy ground; with each step you walk the path of love. Feeling a reverence for life in all its forms, you see each form as perfect and sacred just as it is. Even the ground beneath your feet, the soil, the stones, and the grass are holy. You see the love of God in each and every face, including your own face. Like standing in sunlight, you are bathed in the glorious light of love. Your heart opens like a flower and your life blossoms beyond your wildest expectation.

For centuries the Hopi Indians have cultivated corn and conducted every aspect of their daily lives with an awareness of the sacred nature of all that we do. In his book *Religion and Hopi Life in the Twentieth Century*, John Loftin tells the story of a scholar who asks a Hopi farmer if it's true that the crops would fail if a Hopi just kicks the ground to cover the corn kernels he's planting, instead of

SELFLESS LOVE

carefully and prayerfully using his hand to cover and pat the soil over the kernels. The Hopi replies that he doesn't know whether the crops would fail or not, but that kicking the earth would truly show what kind of a person one is. This story applies not just to Hopis but to all of us. We may not know what the outcomes of our actions will be, but our actions themselves speak volumes about what kind of human beings we are.

Being love flows forth in actions that are respectful toward people, things, and the earth. We do ourselves and others no favors by lowering our standards. One day at the supper table my thirteen-year-old granddaughter, Brenna, was telling us about the terrible way some of the kids at school tease other kids, day after day. She said that the parents of the kids being teased spoke with school officials, who say they have a policy of zero tolerance for bullying, but nothing was done to stop the teasing. My daughter, Clare, commented, "People just don't have any standards anymore." Brenna replied, "You have standards, Mom." Clare responded, "Yes, I do, and you'll be the better for it!" Holding yourself and others to standards of respect and kindness for one another is a step on the way to being a more loving person.

The greatest barrier to being a loving person is a self-centered attitude toward life. A big ego blocks the light of love from warming your own heart and from radiating love to others. An ego that feels inadequate or unlovable will form thick walls of stone around itself and try to protect itself by throwing stones at others. When you lay down the stones you throw at others, allow the walls of stone you build around yourself to crumble, and surrender your illusion of a separate self, then you experience that you are not a thing. You are nothing and this nothing is everything. There is a Zen saying that the many return to the One and that the One returns to the many. When you empty yourself of the illusion of a separate self and let go of all that you do to protect this illusion, you see that you are not separate from the One. This realization enables you to pour out compassion to the many who are right before you and throughout the world.

It is like in Ezekiel 36:26 when the Lord says, "A new heart I will give you, and a new spirit I will put within you; I will remove from your body the heart of stone and give you a heart of flesh." With the stone of the ego and all its defenses removed, a heart of flesh is revealed. This new heart exudes human warmth. And the spirit dwelling within you is the spirit of love.

Being love
Act from that place
Without barriers
No separation at all
Between who helps
And who is helped

Love reaches out
To love

Being love
Share what you are
In ravaged lands
Love against the odds
Love back to life

There Is No Other

SEEING BEYOND the illusion that you are a separate self and experiencing your nonseparation from God, and from all manifestations of God, changes your perspective regarding compassionate action. There is no separate "you" objectifying and helping a separate "other." You see and feel that you are not separate from others, so you naturally try to relieve suffering wherever it occurs— like your hand automatically reaching out to scratch an itch on your leg. You experience your whole body as one organism. If one part itches, another part responds with scratching. Selfless love arises from the realization that the whole universe, including yourself and all of humanity, is the functioning of one God. The whole earth and all beings are one organism. You and the stars and the moon and the whole cosmos are one body. Pain or suffering in one part is felt and responded to without separation.

A well-known Zen question is "What is the sound of one hand clapping?" This question seems nonsensical at first because it takes two hands colliding to make the sound of clapping. However, on a deeper level, this question points us toward the realization that we are one and that there is no separation between sound and silence. Each hand, each person, and each sound is an expression of the whole. Although most people have two hands, and the left hand and the right hand are different from one another, they are both part of the same body. Each and every hand and each and every person is an expression of the great mystery, the one hand that is soundless and at the same time heard in every sound around the world.

Clapping is not a thing; it is an action. It is not static but created moment by moment by repeatedly bringing the hands together. You are not a thing; you are not static. You do not exist independently from all the action taking place within and around you. You do not exist independently of all that is coming together in this time and place to sustain you. You are not separate from the whole.

The one hand is a fitting symbol of compassionate action because compassionate action is not just empathy and voicing your concern; it is actually doing what you can to help. Compassionate action is a hands-on endeavor. Your hands may be on a shovel, steering wheel, dishcloth, person, phone, or keyboard, but they are busy. Selfless love is not passive; it manifests in loving action.

Selfless love is not compassionate action that is generated by a separate "you" residing inside your head and heart. It is not action devised according to your own view of the world, aimed at helping the "other" who is seen as external to yourself. *Selfless* means that there is no gap between you and the whole, between you and other people. In the face of the other you recognize your own face and respond with love to meet the needs of self and other.

With selfless love, you realize that when you help another you simultaneously help yourself. On the morning of Buddha's enlightenment, upon seeing the morning star, he exclaimed, "I, and the great earth and beings, simultaneously achieve the Way!" The "I" in Buddha's exclamation refers to the whole, which is not separate from the earth and all beings. Buddha realized that we are all one and that no one becomes enlightened alone. The great Way is achieved in unity.

Jesus expressed a similar idea in Matthew 25:35–36 when he said, "I was hungry and you gave me food, I was thirsty and you gave me something to drink, I was a stranger and you welcomed me, I was naked and you gave me clothing, I was sick and you took care of me, I was in prison and you visited me." In this passage, the "I" refers to all people; Jesus is expressing his identity with all people everywhere. Each and every person is Christ's body in the world. He is also expressing our identity with all people; we are one body. Compassionate action is experiencing our true identity and acting not only to meet the basic needs of all people for nutritious food, clean water, clothing, shelter, and healthcare, but also meeting the need each of us has for friendship and being welcome.

Sometimes in life we encounter tragic circumstances that cause great sadness or physical pain and we may find ourselves asking, "What did I do to deserve this?" or "Why me?" This kind of thinking adds sorrow to suffering. The

"I" or "me" in these questions is referring to the separate self. The ego demands an accounting. We may feel anger and resentment toward others or toward our self for contributing to this tragedy. We step outside the wider stream and separate from the wholeness and interconnectedness of life. We search for simple answers amid the complex interaction of history, biology, choice, and conditioning that influence our present situation. We move away from others at the very time we need to move toward them, embracing and being embraced by them. In connecting with others and with life itself, we find the strength and resources to face life as it is, not as we think it should be.

In Beata Grant's book *Eminent Nuns* there is a story about a monk who asks Zen Master Ziyong, "Who is the hero among women?" Ziyong replies that each and every person has the sky overhead and the earth under foot. She says that the truth is not upheld by any one person alone and that nobody is a hero apart from the mountains, hills, magpies, crows, flowers, water, earth, and sky. She has seen beyond the sense of a small separate self and beyond the false dichotomy between self and other.

One hot summer day when I was eight years old, I was swimming with my brother, sister, and cousins in Irondequoit Creek. The adults were picnicking on the grassy bank about six feet above the water's edge. I was swimming and splashing and having a good time when suddenly I got a little too far out into the middle of the creek and felt the muddy creek bottom drop off beneath my feet. I sank beneath the water, trying to touch ground with my foot to bounce myself back toward the shore but did not reach bottom. I panicked and started thrashing about trying to keep my head above water but sank several times in the process, thinking "I'm drowning." My uncle Walt glanced down from the bank above and saw that I was in trouble and without hesitation leaped off the bank into the creek. He quickly reached me and carried me to safety.

The time to be a hero is right now. There is no other time. In the blink of an eye opportunity is lost. There is no other place. The place is right here, wherever you are when you notice a need. Respond with what is needed. There is no other action. Just do the work at hand.

A nurse friend of mine recently returned from a mission trip to Haiti. She described an endless line of men, women, and children around the block and down the street outside the clinic, waiting to be seen. At first she felt completely inadequate and overwhelmed, but as she cared for them one by one, she realized that there was no other person to care for than the one in the exam room right at the moment. Working in this way she regained her focus, energy, and ability to be fully present and helpful. There is no other compassionate action, just this.

On his way home from work the other day my nephew, Michael, stopped by to visit his ninety-year-old grandmother-in-law. While they sat at the kitchen table having a cup of tea together, she became incoherent and seemed to be having a stroke. He called 911 and soon the rescue squad arrived to take her to the hospital. When Michael returned home later that evening, his two young daughters gave him a hero's welcome, saying, "You saved Great-Grandma's life!"

There are hundreds of opportunities large and small for compassionate action, but there is no other opportunity than the one right here and now in front of you. After his sister's death, a friend told me about how loving she had been to him, both when he was a little boy and through the years. It made him really sad that her husband didn't treat her well. He said wistfully, "It would have taken so little to make her happy." This was an opportunity lost. The hero does small acts of love to make another happy. There is no other love than this.

The one hand is this hand
There is no other hand
There is no other face
Than the one right in front of you
There is no other time
Than now
There is no other place
Than here
There is no other act of love
Than this small act
There is no stranger
No hero
Apart from this one
There is no other

Selfless Service

S ELFLESS SERVICE is work done for the benefit of the people, the community, all beings, the planet, the whole. *Selfless* means that the work is not done from a narrow, egotistical view of self and reality, but from a broad, unbounded view that appreciates complexity and wholeness. In selfless service the one serving and the one being served are not separate.

Selfless service is collaborative and mutual. It is not doing what you think is best for others; selfless service is helping others accomplish what they view as best for themselves. There is dialogue and participation among all those involved to determine the needs and the best course of action to meet those needs. Gaining multiple perspectives helps prevent negative or unforeseen consequences that may result even from well-intentioned assistance. There is a saying that "The road to hell is paved with good intentions." Even good intentions can result in disastrous effects.

Selfless service requires awareness of your intentions and motivations for helping. Is your primary intention to help people or to advance an economic, political, or religious cause? Selfless service is free of fixed views, opinions, and agendas. Selfless service is not contingent on the conversion of the person you are helping to your point of view and does not require anyone to join your group. You are open to multiple views and opinions and to the realization that these are constantly changing. You reach beyond views and opinions, your own and those of others, to work together as human beings, in order to meet basic human needs that we all share.

In hospitals and health care centers great effort has been exerted to provide continuing education for health care providers to increase their ability to care for patients in ways that are respectful of the patients' cultural backgrounds. Often the term *cultural competence* is used to describe these programs. While the intention to provide culturally appropriate health care is admirable and a step in the right direction, it does not go far enough. A drawback of the cultural competence approach is that it may reinforce cultural stereotyping. In an article in the *Journal of Health Care for the Poor and Underserved*, Melanie Tervalon and Jann Murray-Garcia propose an alternative to the cultural competence approach that they call *cultural humility*. Cultural humility emphasizes a mutually respectful partnership in which the helper does not assume knowledge of the patient's culture but rather acknowledges the complexity of multiple cultural influences that each person experiences. Rather than assuming cultural superiority or expertise, the helper enters the helping relationship as a learner who not only skillfully adapts care to the patient's cultural background but also remains open to learn and benefit from what the patient's culture has to offer to improve healthcare systems or the quality of one's life.

Humility is a key aspect of selfless service. Undertaking selfless service with humility means that you're not acting in a self-serving way for your own glory but to assist, empower, and elevate others—rather than feeding your ego by trying to be the most humble and saintly of all. It is important to be aware of your motivations for serving and what you are gaining from it: the positive feelings that come from helping others; the enhanced self-esteem that results from being a contributor and making a difference in someone's life; the sense of vitality that flows from positive action; the relationships you form with others, including the camaraderie of working with others toward worthwhile goals; the skills you learn through helping; and the approval and recognition you gain from providing valuable service. Selfless service does not mean that you don't gain and grow from the experience. In fact the opposite is true. Selfless service is a mutually empowering experience for both the helper and the one who is being helped. Both learn, heal, grow, and realize the oneness of life.

As part of the application process for acceptance into the nursing school where I teach, the students are required to write an essay about why they want to enter nursing school. In these essays, some students mention their interest in the biological sciences; some describe nurses who were inspiring role models to them; and some tell of serious illnesses they or their family members faced, and the excellent care they did or didn't receive, that lead to their desire to become nurses. The common theme in almost every essay is the student's desire to help people. Additionally, in these difficult economic times, more and more students are mentioning the availability of jobs in nursing. Let me be clear: getting paid a reasonable salary for what you do does not preclude selfless service. In fact, any job, not just helping professions like nursing, can be done with an attitude of selfless service. Selfless service is not so much a matter of what job you do as how you do it. Any job can be done with great love and care so it provides a valuable service to others.

One aspect of selfless service is seeing that no job is too lowly or menial for any of us to do. In the Zen tradition the *tenzo*, or head cook, is a position in the monastery that is held in high esteem. Whereas, in many situations, cooking and running the kitchen are viewed as routine housework or low-level drudgery to be avoided whenever possible. In actuality, it is a vital service that contributes to the health of self and others and to our enjoyment of life. It also enhances a sense of family and friendship. Even a seemingly mundane task is selfless service when done with an eye toward genuinely benefitting others, rather than to the status of the job in society. There is dignity in every job well done. This is another aspect of the humility required for selfless service.

One of the most satisfying aspects of my job as a nursing professor is going the extra mile to help students from other countries. Many of them are from Asia and Africa and they need extra help mastering English at the level required for professional writing and for passing the licensure exam. One student from Nigeria grew up speaking her native language, learned English in school, and then had to learn a third language to get a job in a different district in her country. She was tremendously grateful for the opportunity to come to the United States to get a degree in nursing and dreamed of returning to her country to start a clinic to treat the many people who are infected with HIV in the rural area where she grew up. She was very talented in the clinical setting where her warmth and caring were readily evident to patients in the soft way she spoke with them and in her careful attention to every detail of their care. She got up early in the morning and stayed up late at night to study and complete her assignments. Her determination was an inspiration to me and her fellow students. However, the tests were a great challenge for her. We met frequently to review test questions and to prepare for the licensure exam. When she passed the exam she sent a thank you note, and in it she included a picture of herself back home with her family. I get great satisfaction thinking of all the people in Africa this wonderful young woman will help. Selfless service multiplies itself and reaches out in all directions.

In Matthew 20:26 Jesus said to his disciples, "Whoever wishes to be great among you must be your servant." The greatness that is spoken of in this passage is not referring to any great recognition or acclaim that the servant will receive; it is referring to the great realization of unity, humanity, and love that the servant embodies.

The name my husband received when he became a Zen teacher is Shinkai, which means "Servant of the Servant." When we were in China, Charles stopped at a booth in the marketplace of a village near the Yellow Mountain range to get a stamp carved in stone that he could use to print his name on calligraphies and documents. Our tour guide was translating for him and was having difficulty understanding the meaning of the name so he could translate it properly to the shopkeeper. At one point in the conversation he said, "Oh, I get it, good citizen." Well, somewhat, but what it really means is being the servant of the One who continuously empties out, manifesting love in all of creation.

Humble servant
open to learning.
When you serve others
you discover
they serve you.
Hearts expand
holding each other
in the oneness of life.

Nurturing the Best in Us

THERE IS a wonderful Zen story about a monk who goes to a monastery to practice Zen under the guidance of a well-known Zen master. When the monk meets the Zen master for the first time and requests instruction from him, the master asks, "Have you eaten your rice gruel yet?" The monk replies, "Yes." The master says, "Then wash your bowls." When the Zen master asks the monk about eating rice gruel, he is inquiring as to whether or not the student has seen beyond the illusion of a separate self and experienced ultimate reality. The word "eaten" conveys that this is a direct experience that is nourishing; it is not just the thought of food, which can never be truly satisfying. The rice gruel represents ultimate reality manifesting in each ordinary aspect of life. Can you see this reality and taste it? Are you intimate with ultimate reality manifesting in life itself? If so, go embody this insight in the everyday activities of your life. The Zen master is urging the monk to make his insight move in the world. Go take care of yourself and everyone and everything you encounter. This story encourages us to apply the wisdom we gain to nurture ourselves and others.

One day I was listening to my friend Libby play "Ave Maria" on her oboe and it was so beautiful it brought tears to my eyes. The phrase "Mother of God" came into my mind and I suddenly realized that the phrase applied not just to Mary but to each and every one of us. We are each called to mother and nurture the best in us. When we nurture children we love, we accept them just as they are and, at the same time, help them learn the life lessons they need to be the best they can be. The same applies to nurturing adults.

Many years ago I watched a television interview with Maya Angelou. She told about attending a party at which a person began talking in a very derogatory way about others. She didn't stand by and remain silent; she said to the man, "You can be nobler than that." Her tone was one of positive regard, affirmation, and building on the goodness of people rather than criticism. The way she handled this situation has been an inspiration to me over the years, and it is an excellent example of how we can call forth and nurture the best in ourselves and others. Nurturing is cultivating caring, kindness, respect, honesty, integrity, responsibility, reverence for life, gratitude, joy, and dignity in yourself and others.

In order to nurture others, you need to nurture yourself. This is particularly true when you engage in compassionate action with people who are suffering greatly. When you work closely with people who are experiencing pain, illness, disaster, depression, anxiety, or grief you feel their pain and come face-to-face with your own human

vulnerability. In order to remain engaged and able to provide excellent service, you need to be aware of your own
feelings and needs and find ways to take extra good care
of yourself.

This begins with self-awareness and accepting your
own human limits. You cannot expect yourself to know
everything you need to know to be of service in every situation. You need to acknowledge your need for help and
seek help from others. You are not only a helper but also
one who needs and seeks the help of others.

When you engage in compassionate action or life in
general, you will make mistakes. Mistakes are part of what
it is to be human. I have given workshops on contemplative caregiving for health care providers and a part of the
workshop that is most healing for the participants is sharing their personal stories of mistakes they made in clinical
practice. We talk about the impact of the mistake on the
person and family being cared for; our feelings about the
mistake, which are often intense; what was done to rectify
the mistake and prevent its recurrence; who was hurtful or
helpful in dealing with the mistake; how we coped; what
we learned from the mistake; and how it changed us. For
many of the participants this was the first time they shared
their feelings about making mistakes that harmed other
people and received support from those who had similar
experiences. In being kind toward others who have made
mistakes, you learn the even more difficult task of being
kind to yourself when you make mistakes or do not suc-
ceed in an important task you have undertaken.

Much has been written about burnout, compassion fatigue, empathy fatigue, and secondary trauma among helpers of all kinds, and there is much to be learned from this growing body of knowledge. What many of these overlapping phenomena have in common is emotional and physical exhaustion, which prevents the care provider from continuing to provide sensitive, compassionate service. Self-care is essential to both treat and prevent this deep exhaustion.

Over the years I have been a babysitter, a pediatric nurse, a mother, and a grandmother, and I have learned much about self-care or self-nurture from taking care of two-year-olds. Although a two-year-old will often resist taking a nap or going to bed at night, he or she quickly transforms from an adorable, fun-loving cherub into a grouchy, irritable, crying tyrant when regular naps are missed or bedtime is delayed too long. The need for regular sleep and rest is a human reality at every age. Much of self-care is common sense, like getting regular sleep; napping when needed; eating regular, nutritious meals; exercising; staying well hydrated; and getting regular medical and dental check-ups. Sometimes the burnout or compassion fatigue people experience is just plain old exhaustion from not making time to take good care of yourself. When you take good care of yourself, not only do you benefit yourself, you set a good example that benefits others and you nurture your energy and enthusiasm for life and compassionate action.

A friend, Jan, has been a member of New River Zen

Community since its beginning twenty years ago. Jan is very kindhearted and engages in many different organizations and activities to help people. Jan also loves to run and often enters in 5K races to raise money for worthy causes. In her compassionate action, she has the discipline to prepare herself ahead of time and to pace herself, because she knows she is in it for the long run.

When engaged in compassionate action it is essential to balance the horrors and sadness of life with the goodness and joy of life. Intentionally plan to include pleasure in your schedule each day, as well as taking time to appreciate and enjoy the pleasurable moments that pop up spontaneously. When something funny happens, enjoy laughing with others about it. Simple pleasures to consciously plan into your life might include meeting a friend for dinner, walking in the park, listening to music that inspires or moves you, relaxing with a good book, painting a picture, taking a luxurious bubble bath, getting a massage, or buying a single flower to enjoy. Compassionate action not only includes helping meet the material needs of others, it also means sharing the joy of life. If you find no joy in life, you cannot share it.

When I was in high school, I was on the synchronized swim team. We had lots of fun together practicing and putting on shows. My dad built a swimming pool in our backyard and I spent hours a day during the summer swimming, bedazzled by the sparkling water glistening in the sun. To this day, swimming is my sport. I love to move my body through the water like a fish or mermaid. Some days during the summer I go down to nearby Claytor Lake and float on my back, upheld by the water, gazing into the vast sky above me. This is one of my favorite ways to nurture my body, mind, and spirit and emerge refreshed.

Two of my long-time friends, Roshi Janet Richardson and Sensei Rosalie McQuaide, now in their eighties, are both Zen teachers and Sisters of Saint Joseph of Peace. From them, I learned how to nurture both myself and others simultaneously. They have dedicated their whole lives to selfless service through work with their religious order, the United Nations, and Catholic Relief Services, helping people in parts of the world decimated by war and famine. They were also avid fans of the Notre Dame football team and the Kentucky Derby; we'd often watch those events on television together, sitting on the flowered, overstuffed sofa in the living room of their apartment. Amid loud shouts, cheers, and laughter, they showed me how to play hard and work hard for the well-being of all.

Experiencing the deep peace and silence of meditation is another way to nurture yourself and others to gain the equanimity you need to sustain compassionate action. In meditation you let go of all the thoughts, images, and feelings churning around within you and open to a larger reality that is always vast, calm, and bright. Experiencing calmness and tranquility on a regular basis through daily meditation allows you to stay in touch with this reality even amid crisis, conflict, and turmoil. In this way you become more resilient in riding out the storms of life: your own storms and the storms of others.

In a room full of angels
The flutter of wings
Each feather a prayer
A vision new.

Nurture the infant vision
A small white wish
Fragile and frail
In need of care.

Nurture this dream that comes
In the gentle flutter of angel wings
This infant flame
Without a name
That comes in the night.

Loving the Environment

L OVING AND taking care of the environment is mobi-
lized by seeing and feeling that you are not separate
from the environment. In their biography *Rabindranath
Tagore: The Myriad-Minded Man*, Krishna Dutta and
Andrew Robinson quote from a letter that Tagore wrote
to his niece:

I feel that once upon a time I was at one with the
rest of the earth, that grass grew green upon me,
that the autumn sun fell on me and under its rays
the warm scent of youth wafted from every pore
of my far-flung evergreen body. As my waters and
mountains lay spread out through every land,
dumbly soaking up the radiance of a cloudless sky,
an elixir of life and joy was inarticulately secreted
from the immensity of my being. So it is that my
feelings seem to be those of our ancient planet,
ever germinant and efflorescent, shuddering with
sun-kissed delight. The current of my consciousness streams through each blade of grass, each
sucking root, each sappy vein, and breaks out in

the waving fields of corn and in the rustling leaves
of the palms.

The experience of being one with the earth, which Tagore so beautifully describes, is ecstatic and energizing, like
falling in love with the mountains, rivers, grass, corn, ever-
greens, and palm trees. Despite his eloquent description,
Tagore alludes to the experience being beyond thought
and words. Experiencing that the earth is our body enables
us to give the environment the same loving care we devote
to conserving our own bodily health, vitality, and energy.

Over the years I have been fortunate to visit most of the
national parks across the United States. They are one of
our nation's greatest resources because their wild majesty
nurtures, liberates, and expands the human spirit. Being
out in nature is where many people feel closest to God. If
we fail to preserve this natural resource, the spirit of ourselves and our children will fail to be nurtured, and the
spirit of our nation will die.

It was in the foothills of the Rockies that I first experienced formlessness: my own and the mountains'. Experiencing the complete dissolution of my separate self, I was
transparent, as were the mountains. Not only was there
no separate "me," there were no separate mountains, and
in our formlessness we were one. In fact there was no separation from anything—the sky, the moon, and the farthest star. In the aftermath of this experience, there was
tremendous clarity; my heart was wide open, and I was
fully present with the people I encountered at home and at

work. Ever since then, I have not experienced the mountains, rivers, sky, and stars as separate inanimate objects. Nor have I lost the sense of nonseparation and ability to be fully present with the people I meet in everyday life.

In Zen Master Dogen's Mountains and Rivers Sutra he says of the mountains, "Because they are the self before the appearance of any differences, they are free and unhindered in their actualization." You too are the self before the appearance of any differences, and in this realization you are free and unhindered in actualizing the unique human being that you are.

As a child I grew up in a neighborhood surrounded by woods and fields. I loved playing outdoors and was free to play outside all day as long as I showed up on time for lunch at noon and dinner at six. My brother and I, with neighborhood friends, roamed through the woods, gathering sticks to build forts and catching pollywogs in the frog pond, releasing them before heading home for the day. It's sad that so many children in our society these days can't go outside without close adult supervision because of widespread crimes against children. As a result many children spend hour after hour indoors, watching television or playing video games without enough real-life interaction with grass, trees, animals, and other children. Children need the natural environment in order to learn and grow; the natural environment needs children to grow up experiencing and appreciating their complete interdependence with the earth and all beings. The environment needs children who grow to love and protect her.

Living here in the mountains of southwest Virginia, my grandchildren have been fortunate to go on frequent camping trips in the mountains and along the New River with their family and friends. Recently, my granddaughter told me about a special place the children found along a rocky creek, a circular clearing in the woods. They call it Mother Nature's circle. She and the other children meet up there and sing a song they made up together about Mother Nature's waterfall, Mother Nature's trees, and everything that makes up Mother Nature's circle of life. Swimming in the river, hiking in the woods, and wading in the creek, they are forming a relationship with nature that will benefit both themselves and the environment for many years to come. They are an inspiration to get involved with organizations that make these opportunities available to more children and work toward the preservation of natural environments.

Even in urban areas there is much that can be done to experience our unity with nature. Dave Roper, a retired Virginia Tech physics professor in Blacksburg, Virginia, worked tirelessly, alongside many other volunteers from the community, to build and maintain a large solar greenhouse to house community gardens to grow vegetables during wintertime. One of the greatest joys he has experienced from this endeavor is getting to know people from all over the world who garden there, raising many different kinds of vegetables, cultivated using diverse methods from their native cultures. Community gardens are springing up all over the country and they not only provide fresh local vegetables to eat, they also increase environmental awareness and promote a sense of friendship and collaboration among the gardeners.

One day when I picked my granddaughter up from school, she enthusiastically told me that she got to be the botanist for the week. This meant she got to carry the compost bucket out to the compost pile and she got to water the plants inside and outside the school. At her Montessori school they do many things to promote environmental sustainability, such as bringing cloth napkins in their lunch bags to decrease the use of paper goods. It is important to create learning environments that cultivate concern and love for the earth from an early age onward.

Buddha's environment for meditation was outdoors, sitting under a tree. Before his enlightenment, as he sat all night meditating under the bodhi tree, Mara, the lord of desire, came to tempt, threaten, and attack him. When Buddha did not succumb, Mara challenged Buddha, asking who would be a witness to his worthiness. Buddha reached down and touched the earth, saying, "The earth is my witness." Many Buddha statues depict Buddha with his left hand in the position of meditation and his right hand extended downward touching the earth. Buddha's gesture of touching the earth emphasizes that enlightenment takes place right here on earth when we awaken to the realization that we are one with the earth, all beings, and ultimate reality. From this realization, compassion arises not only for all people but also for the plants, animals, and earth itself.

Deborah McLaughlin, a member of New River Zen Community and a dance professor at Radford University, created in collaboration with other faculty and students a dance/theatre production titled "Eating Appalachia: Selling Out to the Hungry Ghost." Through dance, music, readings, and pictures it portrayed the natural beauty and joy of Appalachia along with the environmental destruction brought about by materialism and greed, both individual and corporate. It was a powerful, artistic appeal to stop mountain top removal mining and its ensuing devastation of the environment in mountain communities. This is a wonderful example of using the arts to awaken people to work together to preserve the natural beauty of the mountains and the purity of the water and air—which is life itself. We are all invited to awaken and bear witness that we and the earth are one.

One body
Mountains and deserts
Rainforests and oceans
Rivers and streams
Like arteries, veins, and capillaries
Carrying vital fluids to every cell
Of every being
Breathing in sky and stars
Luminous heart
Awakens

Coming Together

IN ABOUT 1971, on one of our visits to the Hopi reservation, tribal elder David Monongye invited me, my husband, and two friends, all in our early twenties, into the
kiva for a special ceremony taking place that day. Tribal
leaders from around the country had gathered for the
reading of a prophecy. As we started to enter the kiva, one
of the tribal leaders from New York objected to white people being present, so David told us to wait before entering
the kiva while he went to talk with the elder from New
York. After a few minutes, David returned and motioned
us to enter the kiva and take a seat along the wall with
the others. There was one other white person there, a
middle-aged man we did not know. We listened, spell-
bound, to the dialogue among the tribal leaders. They discussed a stone tablet that had been broken and dispersed
in the distant past. They were now coming together, each
bringing a piece of the stone tablet, so the pieces could be
put back together and the prophecy read.

For me this was a formative experience. It exemplified
the kind of coming together that is needed if the earth and
humanity are to survive. Sitting in the kiva, surrounded

by sand and stone, in the belly of Mother Nature, I was aware that my friend Francine and I were the only women present. Many barriers of gender, race, age, tribe, culture, and religion had been transcended for us to be allowed in, and not excluded.

This meeting in the kiva out in Arizona, many years ago, is an archetype for how we need to come together in our world today for the well-being of all. With increasing globalization, and internet access to information from all the great cultures and religious traditions of the world, there is tremendous potential to gain the wisdom we need to work together for the common good. Now is the time to open our hearts, move beyond boundaries, listen deeply, and learn from one another.

Religion has been, and continues to be, both a unifying and a divisive force among human beings. This is true both within and between religious groups. That is why all the religious traditions have hundreds of denominations and sects. Differences in beliefs caused groups to splinter off and form new groups over and over again down through the ages. We now find ourselves constantly on the brink of war as terrorist factions attack disbelievers among their own people and other tribes and nations. It is essential that we clearly see and acknowledge our tendency to dig in our heels and divide from others in the name of religion. This division needs to be balanced with an appreciation for the unifying potential of religion.

Phyllis Tickle raises two crucial questions regarding religion in our time in her book *The Great Emergence*. The first is "What is human consciousness and/or the humanness of human beings?" Aspects of this issue have been addressed throughout *Selfless Love*—how we must see beyond the separate self to experience ultimate reality, God, or the great mystery. Tickle's second question is "What is the relation of all religions to one another—or, put another way, how can we live responsibly as devout and faithful adherents of one religion in a world of many religions?" As we live in a pluralistic society and global community, how do we respect, learn from, and care for one another without losing the depths and distinct contributions of diverse cultures and religions? How do we cooperate and unite without homogenization? There is richness in the distinctions and differences among different religious traditions that can be lost when attending to the commonalities alone. Differences provide checks and balances when we lean too far in one direction or another.

In her book *Toward an Alternative Theology: Confessions of a Non-Dualist Christian*, Sara Grant urges us not to settle for "a relativist juxtaposition of religions, each offering their own ultimate vision, with no discernible relation or harmony between them." She offers nondualism as an alternative that opens new interpretations of scripture and tradition that transcend and yet appreciate differences. Such new understandings do not come from intellectual reasoning alone; they require deep inquiry and spiritual practice. "Inquiry" is not as simple as asking questions and coming up with answers; it is asking, listening, looking, and abiding in unknowable intimacy.

Each semester an adjunct religious studies professor at the university where I teach brings his class to my home to learn about Buddhism and Zen meditation. I begin with a brief presentation and then instruct the students in sitting and walking meditation. We then enter into two silent meditation periods together, with walking meditation in between. This is followed by time for questions and answers. The students respond very positively to this opportunity for experiential learning. Other weeks during the semester the class goes to such events as a Bar Mitzvah or a puja at a Hindu shrine in the home of two physicians from India. The professor is currently studying for his doctor of ministry degree in interreligious dialogue at Wesley Theological Seminary in Washington, DC. In his openness to people of different faiths, he is a wonderful role model for his students. Courses in religious studies that take the students out to mingle in the multicultural, interreligious world in which we live are much more effective than learning limited to books, the internet, and the classroom.

There is a tremendous value in coming together face-to-face. Each year my husband and I attend the annual meeting of the American Zen Teachers Association, which is an affinity group of Zen teachers from all different branches and lineages of Zen. It is an eye-opening experience to see all the different faces of Zen and to see how much diversity of opinion and practice there is even within this seemingly homogeneous group. During the year the members of the group communicate via an email listserv and have engaging discussions about a wide variety of topics. However, when we come together, sitting face-to-face in a circle at our annual meetings, sharing our joys and concerns, not only do we come to understand each other better, we come to love one another.

Each semester I take my nursing students for a day at a local ropes course so they can get to know themselves and each other better and learn to work closely as a team. We participate together in a day of activities to learn not only with the mind but also with the whole body and all the senses. This experience helps the students learn to listen carefully to one another, value the ideas of each group member, and support rather than criticize one another. The day's experiences make clear to the students that they each have different strengths and limitations and by working together they can accomplish far more than any of them could accomplish alone. But most of all they are invigorated by having a day of fun together; they're grateful to build the friendships and support they need to make it through nursing school and work effectively as a team in the complex clinical setting.

Meditation can be viewed as a form of experiential learning that involves the whole body and all the senses. When you meditate with a group, you sit straight and tall, side by side, beyond thoughts, words, and ideas. A deep and subtle bond is felt as you sit together in silence, supporting one another in spiritual practice. The body relaxes and the mind and heart open. When I attend interreligious conferences and gatherings, I find that people listen to one another more wholeheartedly, and the group dialogue is deeper, when times of talking are interspersed with periods of silent meditation together. The bond formed by meditating together makes it easier to acknowledge differences and come together in helpful compromise when necessary. In our pluralistic age, meditation is a way to bring people together so scientists, people from different religions, and people of diverse political viewpoints can create a natural bond of unity and love that supports dialogue and cooperation.

Buddha awakens under the Bodhi tree.
Christ dies on the cross.
In the world of thought
Buddhism and Christianity are different.
In my heart
I love both,
as a mother loves her two children.

Being God's Love in the World

HANGING ON THE WALL of the playroom at my daughter's house are two Currier and Ives prints, handed down from my mother, of a little girl and a little boy saying their prayers. At the bottom of the prints are versions of a prayer that I learned as a child. This simple prayer has been passed down from generation to generation and remains just as relevant for today's children, young and old.

> Now I lay me down to sleep
> I pray the Lord my soul to keep
> When in the morning I awake
> Help me the path of love to take.

The first two lines of this prayer remind us that when bedtime arrives we all need to take time for renewing sleep, laying down all of our cares and concerns and resting completely in awareness of a reality much greater than our small, limited selves. The next line calls to mind not just the miracle of our literal waking up each morning, and the fresh start each day offers, but also our awakening to the realization that we are not separate, isolated entities—to the realization that we are each a manifestation of God's love. This realization leads to the final step of our spiritual path, which is to embody God's love in the world. This is the challenge we all face daily in life, to walk the path of love, one day at a time, step by step for the rest of our lives. Whether you walk the Taoist way, the Hopi way, the Jewish way, the Christian way, the Islamic way, the Hindu way, the Buddhist way, or the way of any other tradition or combination of traditions, you walk the path of love united with everyone. All paths unite in the way of love.

In the Mahayana Buddhist tradition, the highest ideal is the bodhisattva. The bodhisattva is a person or being who has realized the wisdom of his or her nonseparation from ultimate reality and all beings, and then, rather than entering nirvana, chooses to remain in the world, engaging in compassionate action to liberate all beings from suffering, persevering until the grass itself is enlightened. The bodhisattva walks the path of selfless love for all beings.

In the Christian tradition, there is the ideal of the kingdom of God. As Brian McLaren points out in his book *A New Kind of Christianity*, the metaphor of the kingdom of God, where all tears will be wiped away and love will prevail, has often been misinterpreted to mean heaven, a place we will go after death if we are good. Instead, the "kingdom of God" really refers to living a life of love right here and now. Walking the path of love not only transforms your own life but also establishes God's kingdom of love right here on earth through preserving the beauty of the natural environment, sharing the material resources of the world with everyone, and making peace, not war.

Peacemaking requires far more resources, creativity, energy, and love than we have put into it so far as individuals, groups, and nations. Peacemaking requires meeting the physical and spiritual needs of all the people of the world, and so averting the crises of war that burst forth. Peacemaking crosses racial, religious, economic, political, and national boundaries, uniting people face-to-face and heart-to-heart. It requires people working together at home and around the world until every heart feels love and overflows with love for others.

Roshi Bernie Glassman, cofounder of the Zen Peacemaker Order, regularly leads street retreats in large cities where participants spend a weekend or a week meditating together in parks while living homeless in the streets. The participants experience the harsh realities of being too cold or hot, not having ready access to a bathroom, being unwelcome, endlessly moving on foot from place to place, and eating whatever the kindness of someone's heart prepares and offers to the homeless. Street retreats are a way to meet the homeless face-to face in their own reality, bear witness to their suffering, and offer love and support.

In the New River Valley where I live, which is a more rural setting, a coalition of local churches developed a program called To Our House to offer food, housing, and love to homeless men in the area during the cold winter months. The men sleep on cots in one of the participating churches, with each church serving for a week at a time to provide hospitality and overnight supervision. Members of the congregation and neighboring congregations prepare the meals and provide social activities during the evenings. This collaborative program is one way to actually see, rather than look past, human beings in need, and to respond in a creative, open-hearted way.

As we experience the graying of our population, a growing group of people in need of love is the elderly living alone at home or in nursing homes. We need to visit elderly people in our neighborhood to check on them regularly to be sure they are okay, assist with jobs they are too frail to do for themselves anymore, help with transportation when they are no longer able to drive, and most of all listen to them so they know that they are not alone. We all need to reach out in love until no one sits in the hallway of a nursing home feeling abandoned or lonely.

One day I went to visit my mother, who was in a nursing home for the last year and a half of her life. As I walked down the long hallway to my mother's room, a woman in her nineties came up to me and asked who I was and what I was doing there. I told her, "My name is Ellen and I'm here to visit my mother." She said, "I don't have a mother anymore." I said, "I bet you miss her. You can come visit my mother with me if you like." So she did.

My mother's suitemate in the nursing home was always in her bed or sitting in a chair since she could no longer walk. She never spoke to me even though I greeted her each time I saw her. When my brother and sister came down from New York to visit my mother, my brother brought his autoharp so we could sing folk songs together, which my mother thoroughly enjoyed. After singing a dozen songs or more, my brother packed up his autoharp and he and my sister gave Mama a kiss goodbye. As we walked past the suitemate on our way out the door, she peeked her head out from under the covers and in a clear sweet voice said, "More music please!"

I often share the moving short story "Blankets" by Sherman Alexie, a Coeur d'Alene Indian and my favorite writer, with my nursing students. "Blankets" is about his experience spending time with his father in the hospital just after his father had his right foot and several toes on his left foot amputated. It is a heartbreaking yet at times humorous commentary on dehumanizing hospital environments, seen through a multicultural lens. As the story ends, he and his father are singing a healing song together in the hospital hallway while the previously aloof staff members admire their humanity, spirituality, and love for one another despite the harsh realities of their lives.

After reading this story together, I ask the nursing students if they ever sang a healing song for or with any of their patients. One young man said he sang the song "Heroes" to a woman recovering from a stroke at a rehabilitation center where he worked during the summer. He said she loved it and her face and whole demeanor brightened as he sang. Another student told about singing "Jingle Bells" as she and the other rescue squad members worked to get a person out of a wrecked car beside the highway on a snowy Christmas Eve. She said the singing eased the tension of both the patient and the crew who sang along with her. An older nurse said she sometimes sings "Amazing Grace" to her patients. The class asked her to sing it for them, and indeed it was a healing song. Her incredible voice echoed through the building and out into the surrounding hills. Selfless love is like a healing song, transforming your life and expanding your heart while simultaneously healing the hearts of others.

Selfless love, as presented in this book, can be found in the teachings of nonduality included in all the great religious traditions. Nonduality is the moment-by-moment experience that you are not separate from God, others, and the earth. These teachings unite people within and across traditions, allowing us to appreciate differences while embracing the oneness of life. They are an invitation extended to everyone to live a life of selfless love, serving humanity, all beings, and the earth through compassionate action that restores balance, peace, and joy to our world.

Like children playing in the park
Bright colors swirling
Squealing with delight
Falling down in grassy fields
Getting back up to run some more
Glistening love
Begins anew!

Acknowledgments

I AM ESPECIALLY GRATEFUL TO my husband Charles, who read, discussed, and made suggestions that improved every section of this book. His love and companionship make life and book writing lively.

Gyorgyi Voros, who teaches creative writing at Virginia Tech and is a poet and member of New River Zen Community, coached me in writing the verses at the end of each chapter. I am very thankful for her wonderful way of teaching—which includes lots of encouragement.

My Zen teacher Roshi Robert Jinsen Kennedy read the manuscript with both a Zen and Jesuit eye and gave me valuable input that greatly enhanced the book. I really appreciate his ongoing support and inspiration.

I thank my editor Laura Cunningham, whose careful editing added clarity and polish to the manuscript.

Thanks to all the members of New River Zen Community, whose practice supports my practice and embodies the ideas presented in this book. I also thank the members of my church family at Grove United Methodist Church. Their many good works, large and small, are a constant source of inspiration.

Finally, I acknowledge my daughter Clare, son-in-law Troy, and grandchildren Matthew, Brenna, and Elise, who bring so much love, joy, and energy to my life. They keep me young and up with the times.

Bibliography

Alexie, Sherman. *War Dances*. New York: Grove Press, 2010.

Austin, James H. *Meditating Selflessly: Practical Neural Zen*. Cambridge, MA: MIT Press, 2011.

Beck, Charlotte Joko. *Nothing Special: Living Zen*. San Francisco: Harper, 1993.

Brooks, David. "The Neural Buddhists." *New York Times*. May 13, 2008.

Chiesa, Alberto, Raffaella Calati, and Alessandro Serretti. "Does Mindfulness Training Improve Cognitive Abilities: A Systematic Review of Neuropsychological Findings." *Clinical Psychology Review 31* (2011): 449–64.

Cook, Francis Dojun, trans. *The Record of Transmitting the Light: Zen Master Keizan's Denkoroku*. Boston: Wisdom Publications, 2003.

Dutta, Krishna, and Andrew Robinson. *Rabindranath Tagore: The Myriad-Minded Man*. New York: St. Martin's Press, 1995.

Epstein, Mark. *Thoughts without a Thinker: Psychotherapy from a Buddhist Perspective*. New York: Basic Books, 1995.

Foley, Leonard, and Pat McCloskey. *Saint of the Day: Lives, Lessons and Feasts*. 6th rev. ed. Cincinnati, OH: St. Anthony Messenger Press, 2009.

Fromm, Erich. *The Art of Loving*. New York: Harper & Row, 1962.

Grant, Beata. *Eminent Nuns: Women Chan Masters of Seventeenth-Century China*. Honolulu, HI: University of Hawaii Press, 2009.

Grant, Sara. *Toward an Alternative Theology: Confessions of a Non-Dualist Christian*. Bangalore, India: Asian Trading Corporation, 1991.

Hayes, Steven C., Kirk D. Strosahl, and Kelly G. Wilson. *Acceptance and Commitment Therapy*. New York: Guilford, 2012.

Howard, Beth. "Age-Proof Your Brain: Ten Easy Ways to Keep Your Mind Fit Forever." *AARP: The Magazine*. February/March 2012. http:// www.aarp.org/health/brain-health/info-01-2012/boost-brain-health.html.

Kennedy, Robert E. *Zen Spirit, Christian Spirit*. New York: Continuum, 1995.

Linehan, Marsha M. *Skills Training Manual for Treating Borderline Personality Disorder*. New York: Guilford, 1993.

Loftin, John. *Religion and Hopi Life in the Twentieth Century*. Bloomington, IN: Indiana University Press, 1991.

Loori, John Daido. *The Way of Mountains and Rivers: Teachings on Zen and the Environment*. Mt. Tremper, NY: Dharma Communications, 2009.

Loori, John Daido, ed. *The Art of Just Sitting: Essential*

Writings on the Zen Practice of Shikantaza. Boston: Wisdom, 2002.

Lutz, Antoine, John D. Dunne, and Richard J. Davidson. "Meditation and the Neuroscience of Consciousness: An Introduction." In *The Cambridge Handbook of Consciousness*, edited by Phillip D. Zelazo, Morris Moscovitch, and Evan Thompson, 499–551. New York: Cambridge University Press, 2007.

McLaren, Brian D. *A New Kind of Christianity: Ten Questions That Are Transforming the Faith.* New York: HarperOne, 2010.

Mitchell, Stephen, trans. *Tao Te Ching: A New English Version.* New York: Harper Perennial, 2006.

Pellauer, Mary D. *Toward a Tradition of Feminist Theology: The Religious Social Thought of Elizabeth Cady Stanton, Susan B. Anthony, and Anna Howard Shaw.* Brooklyn, NY: Carlson, 1991.

Pew Forum on Religion & Public Life. *U. S. Religious Landscape Survey.* June 2008. http://religions.pewforum.org.

Phelan, Josho Pat. "First Moment." *Mindfulness* 2 (2011): 68–70.

Samy, Ama. *Meditation and Therapy: Zen Is Therapeutic, Not Therapy.* 2005. http://www.bodhizendo.org.

Schweig, Graham M. *Bhagavad Gita: The Beloved Lord's Secret Love Song.* San Francisco: Harper, 2007.

Segal, Zindel V., J. Mark G. Williams, and John D. Teasdale. *Mindfulness-Based Cognitive Therapy for*

Depression: A New Approach to Preventing Relapse. New York: Guilford, 2002.

Sekida, Katsuki. *Two Zen Classics: Mumonkan and Hekiganroku.* New York: Weatherhill, 1977.

Senauke, Hozan Alan. *Shodo Harada Roshi: Nuclear Reactor Zen.* 2006. http://www.thebuddhadharma.com/web-archive/2006/12/1/shodo-harada-roshi-nuclear-reactor-zen.html.

Shaw, Anna Howard. *The Story of a Pioneer.* New York: Harper, 1915.

Soeng, Mu. *Trust in Mind: The Rebellion of Chinese Zen.* Boston: Wisdom Publications, 2004.

Tanahashi, Kazuaki, and Tensho David Schneider, eds. *Essential Zen.* Edison, NJ: Castle Books, 1994.

Tatz, Mark, trans. *The Skill in Means (Upayakausalya) Sutra.* Delhi, India: Motilal Banarsidass Publishers, 1994.

Tervalon, Melanie, and Jann Murray-Garcia. "Cultural Humility versus Cultural Competence: A Critical Distinction in Defining Physician Training Outcomes in Multicultural Education." *Journal of Health Care for the Poor and Underserved* 9, no. 2 (1998): 117–25.

Tickle, Phyllis. *The Great Emergence: How Christianity Is Changing and Why.* Grand Rapids, MI: Baker Books, 2008.

Todres, Les. *Embodied Enquiry: Phenomenological Touchstones for Research, Psychotherapy and Spirituality.* Houndmills, UK: Palgrave Macmillan, 2007.

Wick, Gerry Shishin. *The Book of Equanimity: Illuminat-*

ing Classic Zen Koans. Boston: Wisdom Publications, 2005.

World Health Organization. *The Global Burden of Disease: 2004 Update.* 2008. http://www.who.int.

Yamada, Koun. *Gateless Gate.* Tucson: University of Arizona Press, 1990.

Yeager, M., producer. *The Man on Cloud Mountain: A Video Documentary on Shodo Harada Roshi.* Seattle, WA: KnowledgePath Video, 1991. Videocassette.

Index

Note: Page numbers in italics indicate end-of-chapter verses.

Beck, Joko, 105
bedtime prayer, 205–6
being love, 163–67, *167–68,* 205–11.
    See also embodying love
best friend story, 62–63
Beyond . . ., 94
Bhagavad Gita on compassionate
    action, 138–39
"Blankets" (Alexie), 209
Bodhidharma and Emperor
    Wu, 87
bodhisattva ideal, 206
the body: awareness of, 143–44;
    meditation and, 141–42;
    ultimate reality as manifested
    in, 145–46. *See also* embodying
    . . .
body image, 26, 143
boundaries, 48–50, 158–59
Boundless expanded vision . . . , 128
"a boundless field of benefac-
    tion," 108
brain areas activated during
    meditation, 19
breaks, taking, 159
breathing during meditation,
    17, 39
Brooks, David, 104
Buddha, 160, 171, 195
*Buddha awakens . . . Christ dies
    . . . , 204*
Buddhist organizations: recogni-
    tion of women in, 118–19
Buddhist uses of "God," 104–5
Buddhist views of ultimate real-
    ity, 78, 79–80

Buddhists, Neural, 104
burnout, 155–56, 186

C
caring environments: setting up,
    133–34
caring for yourself, 183–88, *189*
center of yourself, 27–28; life as
    beyond, 99
Charles (husband of author),
    144, 159, 182
child of God image, 90
childlike delight in life, 150
children: and the natural envi-
    ronment, 193–94, 195
". . . Christ lives in me . . . ," 79
"Christ loving himself, one," 83
Christian views of ultimate real-
    ity, 78, 144, 201–2
Christians: meditation experi-
    ence, 78–79, 86
cleaning house, 10
clinging, 45–46
cognitive therapy, 32–33; MBCT,
    8, 33–34
coming together, 199–204
community gardens, 194–95
compassion, 135, 195
compassionate action, *4;* being
    love, 163–67, *167–68,* 205–11;
    Bhagavad Gita on, 138–39;
    bodhisattva ideal, 206; as "just
    this," 173; reverence for life
    and, 165–66; seeing through
    the separate self illusion and,
    169–75; selfless service, 177–82;

sensations during, 34, 35–36, 39; and sensitivity, 149–50; *Sitting silent and still . . . , 43;* spirituality, 103–6; thoughts/thinking during, 17–19, 31–32, 34, 36, 39–40; walking meditation, 141–42. *See also* prayer

meditation space, 21

menial work, 180

mental hoarding, 10

mental projections of God, 90

mindfulness, 8. *See also* awareness

mindfulness skills in DBT, 41–43

Mindfulness-Based Cognitive Therapy (MBCT), 8, 33–34

mindfulness-based therapies, 8–9, 33–34; DBT skills, 41–43

mistakes, making, 185

monitoring during meditation, 40

Monongye, David, 85–86, 199

moon image, 125

moonlight and pond image, 97–98

"Mother of God" phrase, 184

mother-bear mode, 131–32

mountain top removal theatre production, 196

mountains: Dogen on, 193

mundane tasks, 180

Murray-Garcia, Jann, 178

music as imagery, 92

. . . mystery . . . , 100

N

national parks, 192

Native Americans: Navajo ceremonies, 69–70; view of ultimate reality, 138. *See also* the Hopi way

nature. *See* the environment

Navajo ceremonies, 69–70

negation approach, 76

Neural Buddhists, 104

new heart and spirit passage, 167

no droplet forgotten verse (Loori), 80

No imitation . . . , 72

no self, 25–30, 156. *See also* self; selflessness

no witness/observer, 39–43

non-Buddhist story, 119

nonduality (nondualism), 53, 71–72, 210; Christian experience, 78–79; scriptural/religious interpretations, 201–2, 210; and selfless love, 210

nonseparation, 45–51

not knowing, 3, 77–78, 97–100, *100;* and humility, 132

"not one, not two," 53, 58

"not the same, not different," 53–58

"Not this, not this," 76

"Now I lay me down to sleep . . . ," 205–6

Now I'll be silent . . . , 22

nurturing yourself, 10–11, 183–88, *189*

O

observing: DBT skill, 41, 42; no witness/observer, 39–43

One body . . . , 197

"one Christ loving himself," 83

... One face ... As many ... , 58

one hand clapping question, 169–70

The one hand is this hand ... , 175

oneness with the earth experiences, 191–93, 195

ongoing practice, 3

open awareness (clear-eyed awareness), 20, 48, 56, 123

open-awareness meditation and focused-attention meditation, 19–20

original dwelling place, 111

original face question, 91

original self, 28–29, 91

others: identity with all people, 171; insight into selflessness and, 157–58; "There is no other," 169–74, *175;* worry/anxiety about, 156. *See also* connecting with others; helping others

P

pain of separation, 45, 51

paradox of nonseparation, 48

parents' love, 127, 129

participating (DBT skill), 41–43

the particular: human affection as for, 64; and the universal, 53–55; "I am" and "I AM," 67, 68–69

the path of love, 206. *See also* being love

Paul, Saint, 79

peacemaking, 207

perfectionism, 69

Phelan, Josho Pat, 40

picking and choosing, 70, 71

possessiveness, 26–27

posture during meditation, 15–17

practice (spiritual practice): inquiry, 201–2; ongoing, 3. *See also* daily meditation practice

prayer: life with, 2; meditation as, 7, 20, 91–92; Navajo ceremonies, 69–70; "Now I lay me down to sleep ... ," 205–6. *See also* meditation

presence, 21, *88,* 107–11, *111;* compassionate action as, 164; as emptiness, 109–10; of God, 84–85, 95–97, 98–99; of Mary, 11; meditation and, 9–10, 10–11, 107; in psychotherapy, 9, 109. *See also* awareness

Psalms: passages from, 110, 111

psychological development and spiritual development, 109

psychotherapists: meditation for, 9, 109

psychotherapy: meditation and, 8–9, 33–34, 109; presence in, 9, 109; spirituality in, 102–3. *See also* mindfulness-based therapies

R

realization. *See* enlightenment; insight into selflessness

relieving suffering, 169. *See also*

About the Author

ELLEN BIRX has a PhD in psychiatric nursing and for the past twenty-eight years has been a professor at Radford University. She is a Zen teacher and cofounder of New River Zen Community (www.newriverzen.org). She is a member of the White Plum Asanga and the American Zen Teachers Association. She is the author of *Healing Zen* and the coauthor, along with her husband, of *Waking Up Together.*

Waking Up Together

Intimate Partnership on the Spiritual Path
Ellen Jikai Birx
Charles Shinkai Birx
$16.95 | 256 pages
9780961713950 | eISBN 978-1-61429-139-8

About Wisdom Publications

W ISDOM PUBLICATIONS is the leading publisher of contemporary and classic Buddhist books and practical works on mindfulness. Publishing books from all major Buddhist traditions, Wisdom is a nonprofit charitable organization dedicated to cultivating Buddhist voices the world over, advancing critical scholarship, and preserving and sharing Buddhist literary culture.

To learn more about us or to explore our other books, please visit our website at www.wisdompubs.org. You can subscribe to our e-newsletter or request our print catalog online, or by writing to:

Wisdom Publications
199 Elm Street
Somerville, Massachusetts 02144 USA
617-776-7416, or info@wisdompubs.org.

Wisdom is a 501(c)(3) organization, and donations in support of our mission are tax deductible.

Wisdom Publications is affiliated with the Foundation for the Preservation of the Mahayana Tradition (FPMT).